# WHAT IS MAN?

*Mark Twain*

# WHAT IS MAN?

WITHDRAWN

## AND OTHER IRREVERENT ESSAYS
### EDITED WITH AN INTRODUCTION BY S. T. JOSHI

**Prometheus Books**

59 John Glenn Drive
Amherst, New York 14228-2119

Published 2009 by Prometheus Books

Inquiries should be addressed to
Prometheus Books
59 John Glenn Drive
Amherst, New York 14228–2119
VOICE: 716–691–0133, ext. 210
FAX: 716–691–0137
WWW.PROMETHEUSBOOKS.COM

13  12  11  10  09      5  4  3  2  1

Library of Congress Cataloging-in-Publication Data

Twain, Mark, 1835–1910.
     What is man? and other irreverent essays / by Mark Twain ; edited, with an introduction, by S. T. Joshi.
         p.  cm.
     ISBN 978–1–59102–685–3 (pbk.)
     I. Joshi, S. T., 1958–. II Title.

PS1302.J67 2008
814'.4—dc22

2008034195

Printed in the United States on acid-free paper

# CONTENTS

# INTRODUCTION

*T*he conventional portrait of Mark Twain (1835–1910) as a cynical mocker of religion—especially in the late works of his "dark" period, notably *The Mysterious Stranger*—envisions him as a kind of nineteenth-century American offshoot of Voltaire, whose work is enlivened with the same stinging wit, iconoclastic fervor, and irreverent banter as that of his French counterpart, and who masked his deeply felt indignation at religious obscurantism and hypocrisy under a scintillating barrage of raillery and satire.

In recent years, however, some Twain scholars, distressed at the prevalence of this image and disagreeing with those who have maintained that Twain may actually have become a full-fledged atheist, or at the very least an agnostic, toward the end of his life, have been strenuously putting forth a different picture of Twain—a picture of a man who was deeply engaged in both religious doctrine and religious practice, who never renounced faith in God, who maintained deeply abiding friendships with prominent clergymen, and whose burning hatred of injustice and cruelty was fundamentally religious in nature. One scholar has even gone so far as to maintain that the conventional portrait of Twain is the product of an antireligious bias among academicians.[1] While we will find that this revisionist portrayal is not without its merits (and, in fact, is not necessarily in conflict with the image of Twain as a religious satirist), it seems on the whole a highly tendentious argument designed to whitewash Twain and to brush some of his more pungent lampoonings of religion—and specifically Christianity—under the rug. In any case, the keenness—and, at times, the vitriol—of Twain's criticism of religion makes him at the very least a dubious ally of the devout. With friends like Twain, religion doesn't need any enemies.

There is, of course, no question of Samuel Langhorne Clemens's saturation in the Christian religion from an early age. He was raised as a Presbyterian and no doubt accepted the stern precepts of the Westminster Catechism, although there is evidence that his own father, Marshall Clemens, was not a full believer.[2] His mother, Jane Clemens, was unquestionably devout, but her broad-minded and undogmatic faith stressed the role of religion in relieving social ills and injustices, and there is no doubt that the mature Twain's devotion to these same principles was initially a result of his mother's influence. Sam attended church and Sunday school faithfully as a boy, and his letters and other writings are filled with vivid memories of church services. Twain's writings also display his thorough familiarity with the central texts of the Bible.

And yet by the age of fourteen Twain had already become something of a skeptic. Around 1858, when he was a pilot on a riverboat on the Mississippi, he was fired up by Thomas Paine's *The Age of Reason*—which displayed exactly the same fury at the cavernous gap between religious doctrine and religious practice that Twain himself would later emphasize. Twain would also later read that monumental polemic Andrew D. White's *A History of the Warfare of Science with Theology in Christendom* (1896).

Twain's views on religion were markedly influenced by his marriage to Olivia (Livy) Langdon, of Elmira, New York. The Langdons were liberal Presbyterians opposed to slavery and devoted to the social gospel. It does appear that, under Livy's influence, Twain became more religiously observant; it was also at this time that he became friends with the Beecher family (especially Thomas Beecher, a longtime pastor in Elmira) and with Joseph Twichell, pastor of the Asylum Church in Hartford, Connecticut. But Twain told both Livy and Twichell that he frankly disbelieved in the divine inspiration of the Bible, so it is hardly accurate to say that their influence inclined Twain toward greater religious orthodoxy.

It has been maintained that Twain's "animus was not so much against religion as it was against the institutions that controlled the religious spirit. His virulent attacks are upon the hypocrites who appropriate the language of religion to achieve an irreligious end."[3] We will find that this is a serious misconstrual of Twain's views, especially as they evolved toward the end of his life; but some of his earlier writings do focus on these matters. "About Smells" (1870) pointedly criticizes a fastidious pastor who did not wish working-class people (who might not have bathed recently) to occupy the pews of their wealthier neighbors. "The Indignity Put upon the Remains of George Holland by the Rev. Mr. Sabine" (1871) takes to task another clergyman who refused to preside over the funeral of an actor—a member of a profession in very low social and moral standing at the time. "The Revised Catechism" (1871) suggests that money has become the core of the American religion (a point made also in his collaborative novel, *The Gilded Age* [1873]). Even the much later squib "Letter from the Recording Angel" (ca. 1885) pungently skewers the niggardly charity of a wealthy acquaintance of purportedly pious demeanor.

But it would be a serious error to think that Twain is criticizing merely the hypocrisy of those whose professed belief in Christianity should make them advocates, rather than opponents, of justice, mercy, and kindness. A series of three untitled statements of belief, written in the 1880s, does indeed begin with the resounding statement "I believe in God the Almighty"; but it quickly proceeds with *disbelief* in the divine inspiration of the Bible ("it not only was not written by God, but was not even written by remarkably capable *men*"), in special providences (the interference of God in human affairs), in eternal punishment (one of Twain's *bêtes noires*), and in a religiously based morality.

Several of these points are worth elaborating. Twain had actually accepted a belief in special providences early as a young boy, and acknowledged the doctrine as late as 1878.[4] But the statements of the 1880s definitively reject the notion—as does "Letter from the Recording Angel," which tartly displays the self-serving nature of prayers for God's intervention in human affairs.

Twain's blunt assertion that "the world's moral laws are the outcome of the world's experience" puts the lie to Harold K. Bush's claim that "the insistence today that a person can indeed be quite 'ethical' even if that person is not 'religious' might have baffled many Americans of the Gilded Age," and that "throughout Twain's life he was 'ethically' a Christian."[5] In fact, it becomes eminently clear that Twain found Christian ethics fundamentally lacking—not merely because they were observed more in speech than in action, but because they were, in their very essence, unsound. The harshly critical essay "Bible Teaching and Religious Practice" (1890) lays bare the fact that the Christian church itself has historically engaged in outrageous moral practices—the ownership of slaves and the persecution of supposed "witches"—and done so because its own scripture unequivocally endorses these practices. It was only the civilizing influence of Western society that forced the church to modify its behavior. In this whole issue Twain appears to have been influenced by a number of British intellectuals—from W. E. H. Lecky to Herbert Spencer to Leslie Stephen—who were working toward a self-supporting theory of morals not tied to religion but based upon the overall good of society and the individuals who compose it.

The doctrines of hell and eternal punishment angered Twain more violently than any other feature of Christian dogma. He may have erred in attributing the doctrines specifically to Jesus—although he is correct in asserting that the Hebrew scriptures contain few if any hints of a hell where the wicked are consigned for all eternity, and also correct in maintaining that Jesus' statements in the synoptic Gospels are rife with references to fire and brimstone. Twain could not ascertain the *purpose* of eternal punishment: it could not possibly be done to rectify the behavior of sinners, for they are not given any opportunity to redeem themselves; and punishment for any other reason is merely a product of hatred and vengeance, something that no morally upright person could attribute to God. As it is, by the 1880s Twain was already coming to doubt the very existence of an afterlife. Late in life he definitively rejected the notion:

I have long ago lost my belief in immortality—also my interest in it. . . . I have sampled this life and it is sufficient. . . . Annihilation has no terrors for me, because I have already tried it before I was born. . . . There was a peace, a serenity, an absence of all sense of responsibility, an absence of worry, an absence of care, grief, perplexity; and the presence of a deep content and unbroken satisfaction in that hundred million years of holiday which I look back upon with a tender longing and with a grateful desire to resume, when the opportunity comes.[6]

It is likely that Twain's skepticism, during the 1880s and 1890s, developed from two distinct causes: his acceptance of the theory of evolution and his absorption of some of the central theses of the "higher criticism" of the Bible. William E. Phipps writes that Twain "was one of the first noted Americans to accept Darwin's theory of evolution. . . . Darwin's views so interested him that he owned thirteen of his books. Marginal notes in his copy of Darwin's *The Descent of Man* show that he read that book carefully."[7] Twain's views on Darwin are exhibited in amusing fashion in two satirical pieces, "The Character of Man" (1885) and "Man's Place in the Animal World" (1896). Both essays firmly place humanity within the spectrum of sentient life on this planet, but the latter wittily declares that Darwin is wrong on one point: it is not that the human race has *ascended* from the "lower" animals, but has in fact declined. For it is only the human being who is greedy, vengeful, and hypocritical. "He is the only one that inflicts pain for the pleasure of doing it." He is the only one who enslaves, who is a patriot, who is religious (and this is put forth as a criticism), and who is intolerant of others' beliefs. A pendant to these two pieces, "'Was the World Made for Man?'" (1903), reveals Twain's absorption of contemporary geology: if the world is at least one hundred million years old, as geologists such as Sir Charles Lyell have asserted, why is it that God created humanity so late in the game?

The effect of the "higher criticism"—a movement, initiated by German philologists of the early to mid-nineteenth century, whereby the Bible was scrutinized carefully in terms of its genesis and composition, with the result that many came to doubt that it constituted some kind of stenographic dictation from God—was believed by many in the nineteenth century to be even more of a threat to orthodoxy than evolution or other scientific advances.[8] If the Bible was not God's word, how could it be trusted as a guide to doctrine and conduct?

Twain reflects these doubts in numerous writings, perhaps never more piquantly than in the satire "The Second Advent" (1881). Here, Twain brings the story of the Virgin Birth up to date, laying bare how implausible it would be to believe, merely on the basis of the woman's own testimony and of the "angel" whom she claims to have visited her, that a virgin could have borne a child from God. A much later piece, "As Concerns Interpreting the Deity" (1905), may actually be a satire of the higher criticism in its bogus citations of scholars who have attempted to decipher the Rosetta Stone.

One of the issues that tormented Twain throughout his life was the origin of evil. How could God let evil—whether it take the form of "natural" evils (earthquakes, floods, or pestilence) or "moral" evils (human greed, depravity, or cruelty)—exist? Why is God himself not responsible for these evils, if he created them or created human beings and other creatures who, in performing "evil" actions, are merely obeying the dictates of their nature? Twain emphasizes these points in another pungent satire, "Little Bessie" (1907 or 1908). However implausible it may be to envision a three-year-old asking the difficult questions that come out of her mouth, Twain's point—expressed through the words of an "innocent" who has not been indoctrinated in the acceptance of such an irrational doctrine—is emphatically made. "Thoughts of God" (written in the early 1900s) lays out the conundrum more straightforwardly: If a man invented such a thing as a fly whose spreading of disease among human beings is productive of so much evil, we would certainly condemn him as inexpressibly wicked; so why do we not similarly condemn God? Twain points repeatedly to the irresolvable paradox of assuming a god who is both omnipotent and benevolent. In such a situation, God could relieve all suffering at once. If he cannot do so, he is not omnipotent; if he fails to do so, he is not benevolent.

The standard counterargument among Christians is that God has granted us free will, so that any "sins" we commit become our own responsibility. To this Twain replied bluntly: free will is a myth and an illusion. This is the thrust of the centerpiece of this volume, the philosophical dialogue *What Is Man?* (1906). It may well be true that Twain, in asserting that all human actions without exception are the product of "outside influences," is espousing a kind of "inverted Calvinism" inspired by his Presbyterian upbringing. As William Pellowe has written:

> In the place . . . of the Calvinistic Deity who foreordained some souls to happiness and heaven, and foredoomed others to lives of sin and the

punishment of hell, Twain had put a machine which determined everything which happened on the earth and above it, in the individual's life and in society, thereby being the cause of joy and woe, of respectability and crime, of diseases and war.[9]

But the stance also reveals Twain's thorough absorption of contemporary science and philosophy, which was making more and more evident that our acts are very largely the result of antecedent and circumambient acts on the part of others, and that the standard notion of free will as an uncaused or self-caused action is both inconceivable and paradoxical. Twain also provides, in this long dialogue, a compelling argument against the conventional notion of altruism: no action, however seemingly self-sacrificing, is done save as a salve to one's own psychological comfort. However benevolent and selfless a given act may appear, its prime motivation is the assuaging of our own conscience. "In *all* cases without exception we are absolutely indifferent to another's pain until his sufferings make us uncomfortable." This essay is, in many ways, even more subversive of Christian ethics than many of his other writings, for an acceptance of Twain's doctrine renders any moral approval or disapproval a logical impossibility: putatively "good" actions (as when someone refrains from indiscriminate killing) are so judged merely because they conduce to physical comfort, not because of any intrinsic virtue in them.

Twain's most unrestrained attack upon religion is the late essay "Reflections on Religion" (1906), which, like *The Mysterious Stranger, Letters from the Earth*, and several other documents,[10] was decreed by Twain to be published only after his death. H. L. Mencken criticized Twain for what he took to be a certain pusillanimity in this regard, both as regards these posthumously published pieces and as regards *What Is Man?* which Twain, in a prefatory note to the (anonymous) 1906 edition, admitted he had been working on for twenty-five years. Mencken wrote:

> Mark knew his countrymen. He knew their intense suspicion of ideas, their blind hatred of heterodoxy, their bitter way of dealing with dissenters. He knew how, their pruderies outraged, they would turn upon even the gaudiest hero and roll him in the mud. And knowing, he was

afraid. He "dreaded the disapproval of the people around him." And part of that dread, I suspect, was peculiarly internal. In brief, Mark himself was also an American, and he shared the national horror of the unorthodox. His own speculations always half appalled him. He was not only afraid to utter what he believed; he was even a bit timorous about *believing* what he believed.[11]

These late treatises were written during a particularly difficult period in Twain's life, as he was beset by tragedies both professional (the failure of a business enterprise that led to bankruptcy) and, more significantly, personal (the death of his daughter Susy in 1896, his wife Livy in 1904, and his daughter Jean in 1909). It would, however, be an insult both to Twain's intellect and to his artistic sensibility to argue that it was merely these personal crises that led him to something akin to pessimism and misanthropy. There is very little in these late writings that is not foreshadowed in his earlier work. "Reflections on Religion" does make some spectacularly provocative claims—the Bible reveals God to be "overcharged with evil impulses far beyond the human limit"; the Bible itself "is perhaps the most damnatory biography that exists in print anywhere"—but these barbs are supported by arguments that systematically destroy the very pillars of Christian dogma: God is not a god of mercy; Jesus consigned the great majority of human beings to everlasting punishment; the God of the New Testament is *worse* than the God of the Old Testament, precisely because of this doctrine of hell; the Bible is not even original in its depiction of the Virgin Birth, a feature found in many other scriptures; and Christians are perpetually persecuting others (especially Jews) and fighting wars. This criticism goes far beyond merely the criticism of Christian "institutions." And Twain was no doubt thinking of himself when he wrote: "No Protestant child ever comes clean from association with the Bible."

So did Mark Twain remain a believer even at the end of his life? The question is unanswerable, not least because it is not clear what exactly constituted a "believer" in his day—or, for that matter, in ours. While it certainly may be an exaggeration to say, as Maxwell Geismar did, that Twain was an "eloquent and outraged atheist,"[12] it seems to me that, especially in his later years, Twain was as close to being an agnostic as it is possible to be without actually stating any definite doubt of God's existence. Even if Twain acknowledged the existence of a deity, it was in no sense the Christian deity—for Twain had already discarded such indispensable doctrines as heaven and hell, the Trinity (a doctrine he always regarded as incomprehensible), the religious basis of morality, the Virgin Birth, and so forth. One of his last utterances, "Things a Scotsman Wants to Know" (1909), another rumination on the question "Is God the author of evil?" concludes: "if our Maker *is* all-powerful for good or evil, He is not in His right mind." Does the mere reference to "our Maker" imply an acknowledgment of God's existence? It seems doubtful: Twain is merely engaging in the rhetorical device of accepting a given position (that God is both omnipotent and benevolent) and showing that it leads to an untenable conclusion (that God is insane). It is certainly not a conclusion that any believer would want to accept.

It is easy to pluck individual utterances by Twain, written over many years and for many occasions, to convey a sense of his enduring piety; but the overwhelming majority of his public writings—and, in particular, those of his writings that he deemed too incendiary for publication in his lifetime—betray a scathing condemnation of both the metaphysical and the ethical foundations of the Christian religion and the repeated failings of Christians to live up to the best features of their faith. His criticisms are harsher than those of many actual atheists who would follow in his wake, so that the question of Twain's own beliefs becomes largely moot. Emerging from Twain's tender mercies, religion has few garments left untorn.

—S. T. Joshi

# A NOTE ON THIS EDITION

The texts by Mark Twain in this volume have been taken from a variety of editions and—with the exception of *What Is Man?* which because of its length and importance has been selected to lead off the volume—have been arranged in chronological order by date of writing, as far as can be ascertained. The text of *What Is Man?* derives from the 1917 edition, as the first edition (1906) was slightly abridged. In the essay "The Character of Man," portions crossed out by Twain in the manuscript have been restored, as it appears that Twain omitted these sections because he felt they might be received with hostility. (The essay was in any case not published in Twain's lifetime.)

I have added explanatory notes to elucidate literary, historical, philosophical, and other references in the texts; they are placed at the end of each item. Twain himself included footnotes in some of his works; these have been placed among my own footnotes, appended with the abbreviation [MT].

## NOTES

1. See Harold K. Bush Jr., *Mark Twain and the Spiritual Crisis of His Age* (Tuscaloosa: University of Alabama Press, 2007), p. 5.

2. See William E. Phipps, *Mark Twain's Religion* (Macon, GA: Mercer University Press, 2003), p. 9. Most of my information on Twain's religious upbringing is drawn from this book, which is a far more balanced treatment than Bush's study.

3. John Hays, *Mark Twain and Religion* (New York: Peter Lang, 1989), p. 106.

4. See Phipps, *Mark Twain's Religion*, p. 266.

5. Bush, *Mark Twain and the Spiritual Crisis of His Age*, pp. 15, 17.

6. *The Autobiography of Mark Twain* (1924), cited in Phipps, *Mark Twain's Religion*, p. 304. The statement was written in 1904.

7. Phipps, *Mark Twain's Religion*, p. 284.

8. See Bush, *Mark Twain and the Spiritual Crisis of His Age*, pp. 3–4.

9. William Pellowe, *Mark Twain, Pilgrim from Hannibal* (New York: Hobson, 1945), p. 214.

10. *The Mysterious Stranger*, written between 1897 and 1908, was first published in a corrupt text in 1916. Twain's original version was restored by

William M. Gibson in *Mark Twain's Mysterious Stranger Manuscripts* (Berkeley: University of California Press, 1969). *Letters from the Earth* (written in late 1909) was first published in 1962.

11. H. L. Mencken, "Mark Twain" (*Smart Set*, October 1919), in *H. L. Mencken on American Literature*, ed. S. T. Joshi (Athens: Ohio University Press, 2002), p. 31.

12. Maxwell Geismar, *Mark Twain: An American Prophet* (Boston: Houghton Mifflin, 1970), p. 354.

# WHAT IS MAN?
## (1906)

## I

### A. MAN THE MACHINE    B. PERSONAL MERIT

[The Old Man and the Young Man had been conversing. The Old Man had asserted that the human being is merely a machine, and nothing more. The Young Man objected, and asked him to go into particulars and furnish his reasons for his position.]

OLD MAN. What are the materials of which a steam-engine is made?

YOUNG MAN. Iron, steel, brass, white-metal, and so on.

O. M. Where are these found?

Y. M. In the rocks.

O. M, In a pure state?

Y. M. No—in ores.

O. M. Are the metals suddenly deposited in the ores?

Y. M. No—it is the patient work of countless ages.

O. M. You could make the engine out of the rocks themselves?

Y. M. Yes, a brittle one and not valuable.

O. M. You would not require much, of such an engine as that?

Y. M. No—substantially nothing.

O. M. To make a fine and capable engine, how would you proceed?

Y. M. Drive tunnels and shafts into the hills; blast out the iron ore; crush it, smelt it, reduce it to pig-iron; put some of it through the Bessemer process and make steel of it.[1] Mine and treat and combine the several metals of which brass is made.

O. M. Then?

Y. M. Out of the perfected result, build the fine engine.

O. M. You would require much of this one?

Y. M. Oh, indeed yes.

O. M. It could drive lathes, drills, planers, punches, polishers, in a word all the cunning machines of a great factory?

Y. M. It could.

O. M. What could the stone engine do?

Y. M. Drive a sewing-machine, possibly—nothing more, perhaps.

O. M. Men would admire the other engine and rapturously praise it?

Y. M. Yes.

O. M. But not the stone one?

Y. M. No.

O. M. The merits of the metal machine would be far above those of the stone one?

Y. M. Of course.

O. M. Personal merits?

Y. M. *Personal* merits? How do you mean?

O. M. It would be personally entitled to the credit of its own performance?

Y. M. The engine? Certainly not.

O. M. Why not?

Y. M. Because its performance is not personal. It is a result of the law of its construction. It is not a *merit* that it does the things which it is set to do—it can't *help* doing them.

O. M. And it is not a personal demerit in the stone machine that it does so little?

Y. M. Certainly not. It does no more and no less than the law of its make permits and compels it to do. There is nothing *personal* about it; it cannot choose. In this process of "working up to the matter" is it your idea to work up to the proposition that man and a machine are about the same thing, and that there is no personal merit in the performance of either?

O. M. Yes—but do not be offended; I am meaning no offense. What makes the grand difference between the stone engine and the steel one?

Shall we call it training, education? Shall we call the stone engine a savage and the steel one a civilized man? The original rock contained the stuff of which the steel one was built—but along with it a lot of sulphur and stone and other obstructing inborn heredities, brought down from the old geologic ages—prejudices, let us call them. Prejudices which nothing within the rock itself had either *power* to remove or any *desire* to remove. Will you take note of that phrase?

Y. M. Yes. I have written it down: "Prejudices which nothing within the rock itself had either power to remove or any desire to remove." Go on.

O. M. Prejudices which must be removed by *outside influences* or not at all. Put that down.

Y. M. Very well; "Must be removed by outside influences or not at all." Go on.

O. M. The iron's prejudice against ridding itself of the cumbering rock. To make it more exact, the iron's absolute *indifference* as to whether the rock be removed or not. Then comes the *outside influence* and grinds the rock to powder and sets the ore free. The *iron* in the ore is still captive. An *outside influence* smelts it free of the clogging ore. The iron is emancipated iron, now, but indifferent to further progress. An *outside influence* beguiles it into the Bessemer furnace and refines it into steel of the first quality. It is educated, now—its training is complete. And it has reached its limit. By no possible process can it be educated into *gold*. Will you set that down?

Y. M. Yes. "Everything has its limit—iron ore cannot be educated into gold."

O. M. There are gold men, and tin men, and copper men, and leaden men, and steel men, and so on—and each has the limitations of his nature, his heredities, his training, and his environment. You can build engines out of each of these metals, and they will all perform, but you must not require the weak ones to do equal work with the strong ones. In each case, to get the best results, you must free the metal from its obstructing prejudicial ores by education—smelting, refining, and so forth.

Y. M. You have arrived at man, now?

O. M. Yes. Man the machine—man the impersonal engine. Whatsoever a man is, is due to his make, and to the *influences* brought to bear upon it by his heredities, his habitat, his associations. He is moved, directed, commanded, by *exterior* influences—*solely*. He *originates* nothing, not even a thought.

Y. M. Oh, come! Where did I get my opinion that this which you are talking is all foolishness?

O. M. It is a quite natural opinion—indeed an inevitable opinion—but *you* did not create the materials out of which it is formed. They are odds and ends of thoughts, impressions, feelings, gathered unconsciously from a thousand books, a thousand conversations, and from streams of thought and feeling which have flowed down into your heart and brain out of the hearts and brains of centuries of ancestors. *Personally* you did not create even the smallest microscopic fragment of the materials out of which your opinion is made; and personally you cannot claim even the slender merit of *putting the borrowed materials together*. That was done *automatically*—by your mental machinery, in strict accordance with the law of that machinery's construction. And you not only did not make that machinery yourself, but you have *not even any command over it*.

Y. M. This is too much. You think I could have formed no opinion but that one?

O. M. Spontaneously? No. And *you did not form that one*; your machinery did it for you—automatically and instantly, without reflection or the need of it.

Y. M. Suppose I had reflected? How then?

O. M. Suppose you try?

Y. M. (*After a quarter of an hour.*) I have reflected.

O. M. You mean you have tried to change your opinion—as an experiment?

Y. M. Yes.

O. M. With success?

Y. M. No. It remains the same; it is impossible to change it.

O. M. I am sorry, but you see, yourself, that your mind is merely a machine, nothing more. You have no command over it, it has no command over itself—it is worked *solely from the outside.* That is the law of its make; it is the law of all machines.

Y. M. Can't I *ever* change one of these automatic opinions?

O. M. No. You can't yourself, but *exterior influences* can do it.

Y. M. And exterior ones *only?*

O. M. Yes—exterior ones only.

Y. M. That position is untenable—I may say ludicrously untenable.

O. M. What makes you think so?

Y. M. I don't merely think it, I know it. Suppose I resolve to enter upon a course of thought, and study, and reading, with the deliberate purpose of changing that opinion; and suppose I succeed. *That* is not the work of an exterior impulse, the whole of it is mine and personal: for I originated the project.

O. M. Not a shred of it. *It grew out of this talk with me.* But for that it would never have occurred to you. No man ever originates anything. All his thoughts, all his impulses, come *from the outside.*

Y. M. It's an exasperating subject. The *first* man had original thoughts, anyway; there was nobody to draw from.

O. M. It is a mistake. Adam's thoughts came to him from the outside. *You* have a fear of death. You did not invent that—you got it from outside, from talking and teaching. Adam had no fear of death—none in the world.

Y. M. Yes, he had.

O. M. When he was created?

Y. M. No.

O. M. When, then?

Y. M. When he was threatened with it.

O. M. Then it came from the *outside.* Adam is quite big enough; let us not try to make a god of him. *None but gods have ever had a thought which did not come from the outside.* Adam probably had a good head, but it was of no sort of use to him until it was filled up *from the outside.* He was not able to invent the triflingest little thing with it. He had not a shadow of a notion of the difference between good and evil—he had to get the idea *from the outside.* Neither he nor Eve was able to originate the idea that it was immodest to go naked: the knowledge came in with the apple *from the outside.* A man's brain is so constructed that *it can originate nothing whatever.* It can only use material obtained *outside.* It is merely a machine; and it works automatically, not by will-power. *It has no command over itself, its owner has no command over it.*

Y. M. Well, never mind Adam: but certainly Shakespeare's creations—

O. M. No, you mean Shakespeare's *imitations.* Shakespeare created nothing. He correctly observed, and he marvelously painted. He exactly portrayed people whom *God* had created; but he created none himself. Let us spare him the slander of charging him with trying. Shakespeare could not create. *He was a machine, and machines do not create.*

Y. M. Where *was* his excellence, then?

O. M. In this. He was not a sewing-machine, like you and me; he was a Gobelin loom.[2] The threads and the colors came into him *from the outside*; outside influences, suggestions, *experiences* (reading, seeing plays, playing plays, borrowing ideas, and so on), framed the patterns in his mind and started up its complex and admirable machinery, and *it automatically* turned out that pictured and gorgeous fabric which still compels the astonishment of the world. If Shakespeare had been born and bred on a barren and unvisited rock in the ocean his mighty intellect would have had no *outside material* to work with, and could have invented none; and *no outside influences*, teachings, moldings, persuasions, inspirations, of a valuable sort, and could have invented none; and so Shakespeare would have produced nothing. In Turkey he would have produced something—something up to the highest limit of Turkish influences, associations, and training. In France he would have produced something better—something up to the highest limit of the French influences and training. In England he rose to the highest limit attainable through the *outside helps afforded by that land's ideals, influences, and training.* You and I are but sewing-machines. We must turn out what we can; we must do our endeavor and care nothing at all when the unthinking reproach us for not turning out Gobelins.

Y. M. And so we are mere machines! And machines may not boast, nor feel proud of their performance, nor claim personal merit for it, nor applause and praise. It is an infamous doctrine.

O. M. It isn't a doctrine, it is merely a fact.

Y. M. I suppose, then, there is no more merit in being brave than in being a coward?

O. M. *Personal* merit? No. A brave man does not *create* his bravery. He is entitled to no personal credit for possessing it. It is born to him. A baby born with a billion dollars—where is the personal merit in that? A baby born with nothing—where is the personal demerit in that? The one is fawned upon, admired, worshiped, by sycophants, the other is neglected and despised—where is the sense in it?

Y. M. Sometimes a timid man sets himself the task of conquering his cowardice and becoming brave—and succeeds. What do you say to that?

O. M. That it shows the value of *training in right directions over training in wrong ones.* Inestimably valuable is training, influence, education, in right directions—*training one's self-approbation to elevate its ideals.*

Y. M. But as to merit—the personal merit of the victorious coward's project and achievement?

O. M. There isn't any. In the world's view he is a worthier man than he was before, but *he* didn't achieve the change—the merit of it is not his.

Y. M. Whose, then?

O. M. His *make*, and the influences which wrought upon it from the outside.

Y. M. His make?

O. M. To start with, he was *not* utterly and completely a coward, or the influences would have had nothing to work upon. He was not afraid of a cow, though perhaps of a bull: not afraid of a woman, but afraid of a man. There was something to build upon. There was a *seed.* No seed, no plant. Did he make that seed himself, or was it born in him? It was no merit of *his* that the seed was there.

Y. M. Well, anyway, the idea of *cultivating* it, the resolution to cultivate it, was meritorious, and he originated that.

O. M. He did nothing of the kind. It came whence *all* impulses, good or bad, come—from *outside.* If that timid man had lived all his life in a community of human rabbits, had never read of brave deeds, had never heard speak of them, had never heard any one praise them nor express envy of the heroes that had done them, he would have had no more idea of bravery than Adam had of modesty, and it could never by any possibility have occurred to him to *resolve* to become brave. He *could not originate the idea*—it had to come to him from the *outside*. And so, when he heard bravery extolled and cowardice derided, it woke him up. He was ashamed. Perhaps his sweetheart turned up her nose and said, "I am told that you are a coward!" It was not *he* that turned over the new leaf—she did it for him. *He* must not strut around in the merit of it—it is not his.

Y. M. But, anyway, he reared the plant after she watered the seed.

O. M. No. *Outside influences* reared it. At the command—and trembling—he marched out into the field—with other soldiers and in the daytime, not alone and in the dark. He had the *influence of example*, he drew courage from his comrades' courage; he was afraid, and wanted to run, but he did not dare; he was *afraid* to run, with all those soldiers looking on. He was progressing, you see—the moral fear of shame had risen superior to the physical fear of harm. By the end of the campaign experience will have taught him that not *all* who go into battle get hurt—an outside influence which will be helpful to him; and he will also have learned how sweet it is to be praised for courage and be huzza'd at with tear-choked voices as the war-worn regiment marches past the worshiping multitude with flags flying and the drums beating. After that he will be as securely brave as any veteran in the army—and there will not be a shade nor suggestion of *personal merit* in it anywhere; it will all have come from the *outside*. The Victoria Cross[3] breeds more heroes than—

Y. M. Hang it, where is the sense in his becoming brave if he is to get no credit for it?

O. M. Your question will answer itself presently. It involves an important detail of man's make which we have not yet touched upon.

Y. M. What detail is that?

O. M. The impulse which moves a person to do things—the only impulse that ever moves a person to do a thing.

Y. M. The *only* one! Is there but one?

O. M. That is all. There is only one.

Y. M. Well, certainly that is a strange enough doctrine. What is the sole impulse that ever moves a person to do a thing?

O. M. The impulse to *content his own spirit*—the *necessity* of contenting his own spirit and *winning its approval.*

Y. M. Oh, come, that won't do!

O. M. Why won't it?

Y. M. Because it puts him in the attitude of always looking out for his own comfort and advantage; whereas an unselfish man often does a thing solely for another person's good when it is a positive disadvantage to himself.

O. M. It is a mistake. The act must do *him* good, first; otherwise he will not do it. He may *think* he is doing it solely for the other person's sake, but it is not so; he is contenting his own spirit first—the other person's benefit has to always take *second* place.

Y. M. What a fantastic idea! What becomes of self-sacrifice? Please answer me that.

O. M. What is self-sacrifice?

Y. M. The doing good to another person where no shadow nor suggestion of benefit to one's self can result from it.

# II

## MAN'S SOLE IMPULSE—
## THE SECURING OF HIS OWN APPROVAL

OLD MAN. There have been instances of it—you think?

YOUNG MAN. *Instances?* Millions of them!

O. M. You have not jumped to conclusions? You have examined them—critically?

Y. M. They don't need it: the acts themselves reveal the golden impulse back of them.

O. M. For instance?

Y. M. Well, then, for instance. Take the case in the book here. The man lives three miles up-town. It is bitter cold, snowing hard, midnight. He is about to enter the horse-car when a gray and ragged old woman, a touching picture of misery, puts out her lean hand and begs for rescue from hunger and death. The man finds that he has but a quarter in his pocket, but he does not hesitate: he gives it her and trudges home through the storm. There—it is noble, it is beautiful; its grace is marred by no fleck or blemish or suggestion of self-interest.

O. M. What makes you think that?

Y. M. Pray what else could I think? Do you imagine that there is some other way of looking at it?

O. M. Can you put yourself in the man's place and tell me what he felt and what he thought?

Y. M. Easily. The sight of that suffering old face pierced his generous heart with a sharp pain. He could not bear it. He could endure the three-mile walk in the storm, but he could not endure the tortures his conscience would suffer if he turned his back and left that poor old creature to perish. He would not have been able to sleep, for thinking of it.

O. M. What was his state of mind on his way home?

Y. M. It was a state of joy which only the self-sacrificer knows. His heart sang, he was unconscious of the storm.

O. M. He felt well?

Y. M. One cannot doubt it.

O. M. Very well. Now let us add up the details and see how much he got for his twenty-five cents. Let us try to find out the *real* why of his making the investment. In the first place *he* couldn't bear the pain which the old suffering face gave him. So he was thinking of *his* pain—this good man. He must buy a salve for it; If he did not succor the old woman *his* conscience would torture him all the way home. Thinking of *his* pain again. He must buy relief from that. If he didn't relieve the old woman *he* would not get any sleep. He must buy some sleep—still thinking of *himself*, you see. Thus, to sum up, he bought himself free of a sharp pain in his heart, he bought himself free of the tortures of a waiting conscience, he bought a whole night's sleep—all for twenty-five cents! It should make Wall Street ashamed of itself. On his way home his heart was joyful, and it sang—profit on top of profit! The impulse which moved the man to succor the old woman was—*first*—to *content his own spirit*; secondly to relieve *her* sufferings. Is it your opinion that men's acts proceed from one central and unchanging and inalterable impulse, or from a variety of impulses?

Y. M. From a variety, of course—some high and fine and noble, others not. What is your opinion?

O. M. Then there is but *one* law, source.

Y. M. That both the noblest impulses and the basest proceed from that one source?

O. M. Yes.

Y. M. Will you put that law into words?

O. M. Yes. This is the law, keep it in your mind. *From his cradle to his grave a man never does a single thing which has any* first and foremost *object but one—to secure peace of mind, spiritual comfort, for* himself.

Y. M. Come! He never does anything for any one else's comfort, spiritual or physical?

O. M. No. *Except on those distinct terms*—that it shall *first* secure *his own* spiritual comfort. Otherwise he will not do it.

Y. M. It will be easy to expose the falsity of that proposition.

O. M. For instance?

Y. M. Take that noble passion, love of country, patriotism. A man who loves peace and dreads pain, leaves his pleasant home and his weeping family and marches out to manfully expose himself to hunger, cold, wounds, and death. Is that seeking spiritual comfort?

O. M. He loves peace and dreads pain?

Y. M. Yes.

O. M. Then perhaps there is something that he loves *more* than he loves peace—*the approval of his neighbors and the public.* And perhaps there is something which he dreads more than he dreads pain—the *disapproval* of his neighbors and the public. If he is sensitive to shame he will go to the field—not because his spirit will be *entirely* comfortable there, but because it will be more comfortable there than it would be if he remained at home. He will always do the thing which will bring him the *most* mental comfort—for that is *the sole law of his life.* He leaves the weeping family behind; he is sorry to make them uncomfortable, but not sorry enough to sacrifice his *own* comfort to secure theirs.

Y. M. Do you really believe that mere public opinion could force a timid and peaceful man to—

O. M. Go to war? Yes—public opinion can force some men to do *anything.*

Y. M. *Anything?*

O. M. Yes—anything.

Y. M. I don't believe that. Can it force a right-principled man to do a wrong thing?

O. M. Yes.

Y. M. Can it force a kind man to do a cruel thing?

O. M. Yes.

Y. M. Give an instance.

O. M. Alexander Hamilton was a conspicuously high-principled man. He regarded dueling as wrong, and as opposed to the teachings of religion—but in deference to *public opinion* he fought a duel.[4] He deeply loved his family, but to buy public approval he treacherously deserted them and threw his life away, ungenerously leaving them to lifelong sorrow in order that he might stand well with a foolish world. In the then condition of the public standards of honor he could not have been comfortable with the stigma upon him of having refused to fight. The teachings of religion, his devotion to his family, his kindness of heart, his high principles, all went for nothing when they stood in the way of his spiritual comfort. A man will do *anything,* no matter what it is, *to secure his spiritual comfort*; and he can neither be forced nor persuaded to any act which has not that goal for its object. Hamilton's act was compelled by the inborn necessity of contenting his own spirit; in this it was like all the other acts of his life, and like all the acts of all men's lives. Do you see where the kernel of the matter lies? A man cannot be comfortable without *his own* approval. He will secure the largest share possible of that, at all costs, all sacrifices.

Y. M. A minute ago you said Hamilton fought that duel to get *public* approval.

O. M. I did. By refusing to fight the duel he would have secured his family's approval and a large share of his own; but the public approval was more valuable in his eyes than all other approvals put together—in the earth, or above it; to secure that would furnish him the *most* comfort of mind, the most *self*-approval; so he sacrificed all other values to get it.

Y. M. Some noble souls have refused to fight duels, and have manfully braved the public contempt.

O. M. They acted *according to their make.* They valued their principles and the approval of their families *above* the public approval. They took the thing they valued *most* and let the rest go. They took what would give them the *largest* share of *personal contentment* and *approval*—a man *always* does. Public opinion cannot force that kind of men to go to the wars. When they go it is for other reasons. Other spirit-contenting reasons.

Y. M. Always spirit-contenting reasons?

O. M. There are no others.

Y. M. When a man sacrifices his life to save a little child from a burning building, what do you call that?

O. M. When he does it, it is the law of *his* make. *He* can't bear to see the child in that peril (a man of a different make *could*), and so he tries to save the child, and loses his life. But he has got what he was after—*his own approval.*

Y. M. What do you call Love, Hate, Charity, Revenge, Humanity, Magnanimity, Forgiveness?

O. M. Different results of the one Master Impulse: the necessity of securing one's self-approval. They wear diverse clothes and are subject to diverse moods, but in whatsoever ways they masquerade they are the *same person* all the time. To change the figure, the *compulsion* that moves a man—and there is but the one—is the necessity of securing the contentment of his own spirit. When it stops, the man is dead.

Y. M. This is foolishness. Love—

O. M. Why, love is that impulse, that law, in its most uncompromising form. It will squander life and everything else on its object. Not *primarily* for the object's sake, but for *its own*. When its object is happy *it* is happy—and that is what it is unconsciously after.

Y. M. You do not even except the lofty and gracious passion of mother-love?

O. M. No, *it* is the absolute slave of that law. The mother will go n aked to clothe her child; she will starve that it may have food; suffer torture to save it from pain; die that it may live. She takes a living *pleasure* in making these sacrifices. *She does it for that reward*—that self-approval, that contentment, that peace, that comfort. *She would do it for your child* if she could get the same pay.

Y. M. This is an infernal philosophy of yours.

O. M. It isn't a philosophy, it is a fact.

Y. M. Of course you must admit that there are some acts which—

O. M. No. There is *no* act, large or small, fine or mean, which springs from any motive but the one—the necessity of appeasing and contenting one's own spirit.

Y. M. The world's philanthropists—

O. M. I honor them, I uncover my head to them—from habit and training; but *they* could not know comfort or happiness or self-approval if they did not work and spend for the unfortunate. It makes *them* happy to see others happy; and so with money and labor they buy what they are after—*happiness, self-approval.* Why don't misers do the same thing? Because they can get a thousandfold more happiness by *not* doing it. There is no other reason. They follow the law of their make.

Y. M. What do you say of duty for duty's sake?

O. M. That *it does not exist.* Duties are not performed for duty's *sake*, but because their *neglect* would make the man *uncomfortable.* A man performs but *one* duty—the duty of contenting his spirit, the duty of making himself agreeable to himself. If he can most satisfyingly perform this sole and only duty by *helping* his neighbor, he will do it; if he can most satisfyingly perform it by *swindling* his neighbor, he will do that. But he always looks out for Number One—*first*; the effects upon others are a *secondary* matter. Men pretend to self-sacrifices, but this is a thing which, in the ordinary value of the phrase, *does not exist and has not existed.* A man often honestly *thinks* he is sacrificing himself merely and solely for some one else, but he is deceived; his bottom impulse is to content a requirement of his nature and training, and thus acquire peace for his soul.

Y. M. Apparently, then, all men, both good and bad ones, devote their lives to contenting their consciences?

O. M. Yes. That is a good enough name for it: Conscience—that independent Sovereign, that insolent absolute Monarch inside of a man who is the man's Master. There are all kinds of consciences, because there are all kinds of men. You satisfy an assassin's conscience in one way, a philanthropist's in another, a miser's in another, a burglar's in still another. As a *guide* or incentive to any authoritatively prescribed line of morals or conduct (leaving training out of the account), a man's conscience is totally valueless. I know a kind-hearted Kentuckian whose self-approval was lacking—whose conscience was troubling him, to phrase it with exactness—because he had neglected to kill a certain man—a man whom he had never seen. The stranger had killed this man's friend in a fight, this man's Kentucky training made it a duty to kill the stranger for it. He neglected his duty—kept dodging it, shirking it, putting it off, and his unrelenting conscience kept persecuting him for this conduct. At last, to get ease of mind, comfort, self-approval, he hunted up the stranger and took his life. It was an immense act of self-sacrifice (as per the usual definition), for he did not want to do it, and he never would have done it if he could have bought a contented spirit and an unworried mind at smaller cost. But we are so made that we will pay anything for that contentment—even another man's life.

Y. M. You spoke a moment ago of *trained* consciences. You mean that we are not *born* with consciences competent to guide us aright?

O. M. If we were, children and savages would know right from wrong, and not have to be taught it.

Y. M. But consciences can be *trained*?

O. M. Yes.

Y. M. Of course by parents, teachers, the pulpit, and books.

O. M. Yes—they do their share; they do what they can.

Y. M. And the rest is done by—

O. M. Oh, a million unnoticed influences—for good or bad: influences which work without rest during every waking moment of a man's life, from cradle to grave.

Y. M. You have tabulated these?

O. M. Many of them—yes.

Y. M. Will you read me the result?

O. M. Another time, yes. It would take an hour.

Y. M. A conscience can be trained to shun evil and prefer good?

O. M. Yes.

Y. M. But will prefer it for spirit-contenting reasons only?

O. M. It *can't* be trained to do a thing for any *other* reason. The thing is impossible.

Y. M. There *must* be a genuinely and utterly self-sacrificing act recorded in human history somewhere.

O. M. You are young. You have many years before you. Search one out.

Y. M. It does seem to me that when a man sees a fellow-being struggling in the water and jumps in at the risk of his life to save him—

O. M. Wait. Describe the *man.* Describe the *fellow-being.* State if there is an *audience* present; or if they are *alone.*

Y. M. What have these things to do with the splendid act?

O. M. Very much. Shall we suppose, as a beginning, that the two are alone, in a solitary place, at midnight?

Y. M. If you choose.

O. M. And that the fellow-being is the man's daughter?

Y. M. Well, n-no—make it some one else.

O. M. A filthy, drunken ruffian, then?

Y. M. I see. Circumstances alter cases. I suppose that if there was no audience to observe the act, the man wouldn't perform it.

O. M. But there is here and there a man who *would.* People, for instance, like the man who lost his life trying to save the child from the fire; and the man who gave the needy old woman his twenty-five cents and walked home in the storm—there are here and there men like that who would do it. And why? Because they couldn't bear to see a fellow-being struggling in the water and not jump in and help. It would give *them* pain. They would save the fellow-being on that account. *They wouldn't do it otherwise.* They strictly obey the law which I have been insisting upon. You must remember and always distinguish the people who *can't bear* things from the people who *can*. It will throw light upon a number of apparently "self-sacrificing" cases.

Y. M. Oh, dear, it's all so disgusting.

O. M. Yes. And so true.

Y. M. Come—take the good boy who does things he doesn't want to do, in order to gratify his mother.

O. M. He does seven-tenths of the act because it gratifies *him* to gratify his mother. Throw the bulk of advantage the other way and the good boy would not do the act. He *must* obey the iron law. None can escape it.

Y. M. Well, take the case of a bad boy who—

O. M. You needn't mention it, it is a waste of time. It is no matter about the bad boy's act. Whatever it was, he had a spirit-contenting reason for it. Otherwise you have been misinformed, and he didn't do it.

Y. M. It is very exasperating. A while ago you said that a man's conscience is not a born judge of morals and conduct, but has to be taught and trained. Now I think a conscience can get drowsy and lazy, but I don't think it can go wrong; and if you wake it up—

### A Little Story

O. M. I will tell you a little story:

Once upon a time an Infidel was guest in the house of a Christian widow whose little boy was ill and near to death. The Infidel often watched by the bedside and entertained the boy with talk, and he used these opportunities to satisfy a strong longing of his nature—that desire which is in us all to better other people's condition by having them think as we think. He was successful. But the dying boy, in his last moments, reproached him and said:

"*I believed, and was happy in it; you have taken my belief away, and my com-*

*fort. Now I have nothing left, and I die miserable; for the things which you have told me do not take the place of that which I have lost."*

And the mother, also, reproached the Infidel, and said:

*"My child is forever lost, and my heart is broken. How could you do this cruel thing? We have done you no harm, but only kindness; we made our house your home, you were welcome to all we had, and this our reward."*

The heart of the Infidel was filled with remorse for what he had done, and he said:

*"It was wrong—I see it now; but I was only trying to do him good. In my view he was in error; it seemed my duty to teach him the truth."*

Then the mother said:

*"I had taught him, all his little life, what I believed to be the truth, and in his believing faith both of us were happy. Now he is dead—and lost; and I am miserable. Our faith came down to us through centuries of believing ancestors; what right had you, or any one, to disturb it? Where was your honor, where was your shame?"*

Y. M. He was a miscreant, and deserved death!

O. M. He thought so himself, and said so.

Y. M. Ah—you see, *his conscience was awakened!*

O. M. Yes, his Self-Disapproval was. It *pained* him to see the mother suffer. He was sorry he had done a thing which brought *him* pain. It did not occur to him to think of the mother when he was misteaching the boy, for he was absorbed in providing *pleasure* for himself, then. Providing it by satisfying what he believed to be a call of duty.

Y. M. Call it what you please, it is to me a case of *awakened conscience.* That awakened conscience could never get itself into that species of trouble again. A cure like that is a *permanent* cure.

O. M. Pardon—I had not finished the story. We are creatures of *outside influences*—we originate *nothing* within. Whenever we take a new line of thought and drift into a new line of belief and action, the impulse is *always* suggested from the *outside.* Remorse so preyed upon the Infidel that it dissolved his harshness toward the boy's religion and made him come to regard it with tolerance, next with kindness, for the boy's sake and the mother's. Finally he found himself examining it. From that moment his progress in his new trend was steady and rapid. He became a believing Christian. And now his remorse for having robbed the dying boy of his faith and his salvation was bitterer than ever. It gave him no rest, no peace. He *must* have rest and peace—it is the law of our nature. There seemed but one way to get it; he must devote himself to saving imperiled souls. He became a missionary. He landed in a pagan country ill and helpless. A native widow took him into her humble home and nursed him back to convalescence. Then her young boy was taken hopelessly ill, and the grateful missionary helped her tend him. Here was his first opportunity to repair a part of the wrong done to the other boy by doing a precious service for this one by undermining his foolish faith in his false gods. He was successful. But the dying boy in his last moments reproached him and said:

*"I believed, and was happy in it; you have taken my belief away, and my comfort. Now I have nothing left, and I die miserable; for the things which you have told me do not take the place of that which I have lost."*

And the mother, also, reproached the missionary, and said:

*"My child is forever lost, and my heart is broken. How could you do this cruel thing? We had done you no harm, but only kindness; we made our house your home, you were welcome to all we had, and this is our reward."*

The heart of the missionary was filled with remorse for what he had done, and he said:

*"It was wrong—I see it now; but I was only trying to do him good. In my view he was in error; it seemed my duty to teach him the truth."*

Then the mother said:

*"I had taught him, all his little life, what I believed to be the truth, and in his believing faith both of us were happy. Now he is dead—and lost; and I am miserable. Our faith came down to us through centuries of believing ancestors; what right had you, or any one, to disturb it? Where was your honor, where was your shame?"*

The missionary's anguish of remorse and sense of treachery were as bitter and persecuting and unappeasable, now, as they had been in the former case. The story is finished. What is your comment?

Y. M. The man's conscience was a fool! It was morbid. It didn't know right from wrong.

O. M. I am not sorry to hear you say that. If you grant that one man's conscience doesn't know right from wrong, it is an admission that there are others like it. This single admission pulls down the whole doctrine of infallibility of judgment in consciences. Meantime there is one thing which I ask you to notice.

Y. M. What is that?

O. M. That in both cases the man's *act* gave him no spiritual discomfort, and that he was quite satisfied with it and got pleasure out of it. But afterward when it resulted in *pain* to *him*, he was sorry. Sorry it had inflicted pain upon the others, *but for no reason under the sun except that their pain gave* him *pain.* Our consciences take *no* notice of pain inflicted upon others until it reaches a point where it gives pain to *us.* In *all* cases without exception we are absolutely indifferent to another person's pain until his sufferings make us uncomfortable. Many an infidel would not have been troubled by that Christian mother's distress. Don't you believe that?

Y. M. Yes. You might almost say it of the *average* infidel, I think.

O. M. And many a missionary, sternly fortified by his sense of duty, would not have been troubled by the pagan mother's distress—Jesuit missionaries in Canada in the early French times, for instance; see episodes quoted by Parkman.[5]

Y. M. Well, let us adjourn. Where have we arrived?

O. M. At this. That we (mankind) have ticketed ourselves with a number of qualities to which we have even misleading names. Love, Hate, Charity, Compassion, Avarice, Benevolence, and so on. I mean we attach misleading *meanings* to the names. They are all forms of self-contentment, self-gratification, but the names so disguise them that they distract our attention from the fact. Also we have smuggled a word into the dictionary which ought not to be there at all—Self-Sacrifice. It describes a thing which does not exist. But worst of all, we ignore and never mention the Sole Impulse which dictates and compels a man's every act: the imperious necessity of securing his own approval, in every emergency and at all costs. To it we owe all that we are. It is our breath, our heart, our blood. It is our only spur, our whip, our goad, our only impelling power;

we have no other. Without it we should be mere inert images, corpses; no one would do anything, there would be no progress, the world would stand still. We ought to stand reverently uncovered when the name of that stupendous power is uttered.

Y. M. I am not convinced.

O. M. You will be when you think.

# III

## INSTANCES IN POINT

OLD MAN. Have you given thought to the Gospel of Self-Approval since we talked?

YOUNG MAN. I have.

O. M. It was I that moved you to it. That is to say an *outside influence* moved you to it—not one that originated in your own head. Will you try to keep that in mind and not forget it?

Y. M. Yes. Why?

O. M. Because by and by in one of our talks, I wish to further impress upon you that neither you, nor I, nor any man ever originates a thought in his own head. *The utterer of a thought always utters a second-hand one.*

Y. M. Oh, now—

O. M. Wait. Reserve your remark till we get to that part of our discussion—to-morrow or next day, say. Now, then, have you been considering the proposition that no act is ever born of any but a self-contenting iinpulse—(primarily). You have sought. What have you found?

Y. M. I have not been very fortunate. I have examined many fine and apparently self-sacrificing deeds in romances and biographies, but—

O. M. Under searching analysis the ostensible self-sacrifice disappeared? It naturally would.

Y. M. But here in this novel is one which seems to promise. In the Adirondack woods is a wage-earner and lay preacher in the lumber-camps who is of noble character and deeply religious. An earnest and practical laborer in the New York slums comes up there on vacation—he is leader of a section of the University Settlement.[6] Holme, the lumberman, is fired with a desire to throw away his excellent worldly prospects and go down and save souls on the East Side. He counts it happiness to make this sacrifice for the glory of God and for the cause of Christ. He resigns his place, makes the sacrifice cheerfully, and goes to the East Side and preaches Christ and Him crucified every day and every night to little groups of half-civilized foreign paupers who scoff at him. But he rejoices in the scoffings, since he is suffering them in the great cause of Christ. You have so filled my mind with suspicions that I was constantly expecting to find a hidden questionable impulse back of all this, but I am thankful to say I have failed. This man saw his duty, and for *duty's sake* he sacrificed self and assumed the burden it imposed.

O. M. Is that as far as you have read?

Y. M. Yes.

O. M. Let us read further, presently. Meantime, in sacrificing himself—*not* for the glory of God, *primarily*, as *he* imagined, but *first* to content that exacting and inflexible master within him—*did he sacrifice anybody else?*

Y. M. How do you mean?

O. M. He relinquished a lucrative post and got mere food and lodging in place of it. Had he dependants?

Y. M. Well—yes.

O. M. In what way and to what extent did his self-sacrifice affect *them?*

Y. M. He was the support of a superannuated father. He had a young sister with a remarkable voice—he was giving her a musical education, so that her longing to be self-supporting might be gratified. He was furnishing the money to put a young brother through a polytechnic school and satisfy his desire to become a civil engineer.

O. M. The old father's comforts were now curtailed?

Y. M. Quite seriously. Yes.

O. M. The sister's music-lessons had to stop?

Y. M. Yes.

O. M. The young brother's education—well, an extinguishing blight fell upon that happy dream, and he had to go to sawing wood to support the old father, or something like that?

Y. M. It is about what happened. Yes.

O. M. What a handsome job of self-sacrificing he did do! It seems to me that he sacrificed everybody *except* himself. Haven't I told you that no man *ever* sacrifices himself; that there is no instance of it upon record anywhere; and that when a man's Interior Monarch requires a thing of its slave for either its *momentary* or its *permanent* contentment, that thing must and will be furnished and that command obeyed, no matter who may stand in the way and suffer disaster by it? That man *ruined his family* to please and content his Interior Monarch—

Y. M. And help Christ's cause.

O. M. Yes—*secondly*. Not firstly. *He* thought it was firstly.

Y. M. Very well, have it so, if you will. But it could be that he argued that if he saved a hundred souls in New York—

O. M. The sacrifice of the *family* would be justified by that great profit upon the—the—what shall we call it?

Y. M. Investment?

O. M. Hardly. How would *speculation* do? How would *gamble* do? Not a solitary soul-capture was sure. He played for a possible thirty-three-hundred-per-cent profit. It was *gambling*—with his family for "chips." However, let us see how the game came out. Maybe we can get on the track of the secret original impulse, the *real* impulse, that moved him to so nobly self-sacrifice his family in the Saviour's cause under the superstition that he was sacrificing himself. I will read a chapter or so. . . . Here we have it! It was bound to expose itself sooner or later. He preached to the East-Side rabble a season, then went back to his old dull, obscure life in the lumber-camps *"hurt to the heart, his pride humbled."* Why? Were not his efforts acceptable to the Saviour, for Whom alone they were made? Dear me, that detail is *lost sight of*, is not even referred to, the fact that it started out as a motive is entirely forgotten! Then what is the trouble? The authoress quite innocently and unconsciously gives the whole business away. The trouble was this: this man merely *preached* to the poor; that is not the University Settlement's way; it deals in larger and better things than that, and it did not enthuse over that crude Salvation-Army eloquence. It was courteous to Holme—but cool.

It did not pet him, did not take him to its bosom. *"Perished were all his dreams of distinction, the praise and grateful approval of—"* Of whom? The Saviour? No; the Saviour is not mentioned. Of whom, then? Of *"his fellow-workers."* Why did he want that? Because the Master inside of him wanted it, and would not be content without it. That emphasized sentence quoted above, reveals the secret we have been seeking, the original impulse, the *real* impulse, which moved the obscure and unappreciated Adirondack lumberman to sacrifice his family and go on that crusade to the East Side—which said original impulse was this, to wit: without knowing it *he went there to show a neglected world the large talent that was in him, and rise to distinction.* As I have warned you before, *no* act springs from any but the one law, the one motive. But I pray you, do not accept this law upon my say-so; but diligently examine for yourself. Whenever you read of a self-sacrificing act or hear of one, or of a duty done for *duty's sake*, take it to pieces and look for the *real* motive. It is always there.

Y. M. I do it every day. I cannot help it, now that I have gotten started upon the degrading and exasperating quest. For it is hatefully interesting!—in fact, fascinating is the word. As soon as I come across a golden deed in a book I have to stop and take it apart and examine it, I cannot help myself.

O. M. Have you ever found one that defeated the rule?

Y. M. No—at least, not yet. But take the case of servant-tipping in Europe. You pay the *hotel* for service; you owe the servants *nothing*, yet you pay them besides. Doesn't that defeat it?

O. M. In what way?

Y. M. You are not *obliged* to do it, therefore its source is compassion for their ill-paid condition, and—

O. M. Has that custom ever vexed you, annoyed you, irritated you?

Y. M. Well—yes.

O. M. Still you succumbed to it?

Y. M. Of course.

O. M. Why of course?

Y. M. Well, custom is law, in a way, and laws must be submitted to—everybody recognizes it as a *duty*.

O. M. Then you pay the irritating tax for *duty's* sake?

Y. M. I suppose it amounts to that.

O. M. Then the impulse which moves you to submit to the tax is not *all* compassion, charity, benevolence?

Y. M. Well—perhaps not.

O. M. Is *any* of it?

Y. M. I—perhaps I was too hasty in locating its source.

O. M. Perhaps so. In case you ignored the custom would you get prompt and effective service from the servants?

Y. M. Oh, hear yourself talk! Those European servants? Why, you wouldn't get any at all, to speak of.

O. M. Couldn't *that* work as an impulse to move you to pay the tax?

Y. M. I am not denying it.

O. M. Apparently, then, it is a case of for-duty's-sake with a little self-interest added?

Y. M. Yes, it has the look of it. But here is a point: we pay that tax knowing it to be unjust and an extortion; yet we go away with a pain at the heart if we think we have been stingy with the poor fellows; and we heartily wish we were back again, so that we could do the right thing, and *more* than the right thing, the *generous* thing. I think it will be difficult for you to find any thought of self in that impulse.

O. M. I wonder why you should think so. When you find service charged in the *hotel* bill does it annoy you?

Y. M. No.

O. M. Do you ever complain of the amount of it?

Y. M. No, it would not occur to me.

O. M. The *expense*, then, is not the annoying detail. It is a fixed charge, and you pay it cheerfully, you pay it without a murmur. When you came to pay the servants, how would you like it if each of the men and maids had a fixed charge?

Y. M. Like it? I should rejoice!

O. M. Even if the fixed tax were a shade *more* than you had been in the habit of paying in the form of tips?

Y. M. Indeed, yes!

O. M. Very well, then. As I understand it, it isn't really compassion nor yet duty that moves you to pay the tax, and it isn't the *amount* of the tax that annoys you. Yet *something* annoys you. What is it?

Y. M. Well, the trouble is, you never know *what* to pay, the tax varies so, all over Europe.

O. M. So you have to guess?

Y. M. There is no other way. So you go on thinking and thinking, and calculating and guessing, and consulting with other people and getting their views; and it spoils your sleep nights, and makes you distraught in the daytime, and while you are pretending to look at the sights you are only guessing and guessing and guessing all the time, and being worried and miserable.

O. M. And all about a debt which you don't owe and don't have to pay unless you want to! Strange. What is the purpose of the guessing?

Y. M. To guess out what is right to give them, and not be unfair to any of them.

O. M. It has quite a noble look—taking so much pains and using up so much valuable time in order to be just and fair to a poor servant to whom you owe nothing, but who needs money and is ill paid.

Y. M. I think, myself, that if there is any ungracious motive back of it it will be hard to find.

O. M. How do you know when you have not paid a servant fairly?

Y. M. Why, he is silent; does not thank you. Sometimes he gives you a look that makes you ashamed. You are too proud to rectify your mistake there, with people looking, but afterward you keep on wishing and wishing you *had* done it. My, the shame and the pain of it! Sometimes you see, by the signs, that you have hit it *just right*, and you go away mightily satisfied. Sometimes the man is so effusively thankful that you know you have given him a good deal *more* than was necessary.

O. M. *Necessary?* Necessary for what?

Y. M. To content him.

O. M. How do you feel *then*?

Y. M. Repentant.

O. M. It is my belief that you have *not* been concerning yourself in guessing out his just dues, but only in ciphering out what would *content* him. And I think you had a self-deluding reason for that.

Y. M. What was it?

O. M. If you fell short of what he was expecting and wanting, you would get a look which would *shame you before folk.* That would give you *pain. You*—for you are only working for yourself, not *him.* If you gave him too much you would be *ashamed of yourself* for it, and that would give *you* pain—another case of thinking of *yourself,* protecting yourself, *saving yourself from discomfort.* You never think of the servant once—except to guess out how to get *his approval.* If you get that, you get your *own* approval, and that is the sole and only thing you are after. The Master inside of you is then satisfied, contented, comfortable; there was *no other* thing at stake, as a matter of *first* interest, anywhere in the transaction.

### *Further Instances*

Y. M. Well, to think of it: Self-Sacrifice for others, the grandest thing in man, ruled out! non-existent!

O. M. Are you accusing me of saying that?

Y. M. Why, certainly.

O. M. I haven't said it.

Y. M. What did you say, then?

O. M. That no man has ever sacrificed himself in the common meaning of that phrase—which is, self-sacrifice for another *alone.* Men make daily sacrifices for others, but it is for their own sake *first.* The act must content their own spirit *first.* The other beneficiaries come second.

Y. M. And the same with duty for duty's sake?

O. M. Yes. No man performs a duty for mere duty's sake; the act must content his spirit *first.* He must feel better for *doing* the duty than he would for shirking it. Otherwise he will not do it.

Y. M. Take the case of the *Berkeley Castle.*

O. M. It was a noble duty, greatly performed. Take it to pieces and examine it, if you like.

Y. M. A British troop-ship crowded with soldiers and their wives and children. She struck a rock and began to sink. There was room in the boats for the women and children only. The colonel lined up his regiment on the deck and said "it is our duty to die, that they may be saved." There was no murmur, no protest. The boats carried away the women and children. When the death-moment was come, the colonel and his officers took their several posts, the men stood at shoulder-arms, and so, as on dress-parade, with their flag flying and the drums beating, they went down, a sacrifice to duty for duty's sake. Can you view it as other than that?

O. M. It was something as fine as that, as exalted as that. Could you have remained in those ranks and gone down to your death in that unflinching way?

Y. M. Could I? No, I could not.

O. M. Think. Imagine yourself there, with that watery doom creeping higher and higher around you.

Y. M. I can imagine it. I feel all the horror of it. I could not have endured it, I could not have remained in my place. I know it.

O. M. Why?

Y. M. There is no why about it: I know myself, and I know I couldn't *do* it.

O. M. But it would be your *duty* to do it.

Y. M. Yes, I know—but I couldn't.

O. M. It was more than a thousand men, yet not one of them flinched. Some of them must have been born with your temperament; if they could do that great duty for duty's *sake*, why not you? Don't you know that you could go out and gather together a thousand clerks and mechanics and put them on that deck and ask them to die for duty's sake, and not two dozen of them would stay in the ranks to the end?

Y. M. Yes, I know that.

O. M. But you *train* them, and put them through a campaign or two; then they would be soldiers; soldiers, with a soldier's pride, a soldier's self-respect, a soldier's ideals. They would have to content a *soldier's* spirit then, not a clerk's, not a mechanic's. They could not content that spirit by shirking a soldier's duty, could they?

Y. M. I suppose not.

O. M. Then they would do the duty not for the *duty's* sake, but for their *own* sake—primarily. The *duty* was *just the same*, and just as imperative, when they were clerks, mechanics, raw recruits, but they wouldn't perform it for that. As clerks and mechanics they had other ideals, another spirit to satisfy, and they satisfied it. They *had* to; it is the law. *Training* is potent. Training toward higher and higher, and ever higher ideals is worth any man's thought and labor and diligence.

Y. M. Consider the man who stands by his duty and goes to the stake rather than be recreant to it.

O. M. It is his make and his training. He has to content the spirit that is in him, though it cost him his life. Another man, just as sincerely religious, but of different temperament, will fail of that duty, though recognizing it as a duty, and grieving to be unequal to it: but he must content the spirit that is in him—he cannot help it. He could not perform that duty for duty's *sake*, for that would not content his spirit, and the contenting of his spirit must be looked to *first*. It takes precedence of all other duties.

Y. M. Take the case of a clergyman of stainless private morals who votes for a thief for public office, on his own party's ticket, and against an honest man on the other ticket.

O. M. He has to content his spirit. He has no public morals; he has no private ones, where his party's prosperity is at stake. He will always be true to his make and training.

# IV

## TRAINING

YOUNG MAN. You keep using that word—training. By it do you particularly mean—

OLD MAN. Study, instruction, lectures, sermons? That is a part of it—but not a large part. I mean *all* the outside influences. There are a million of them. From the cradle to the grave, during all his waking hours, the human being is under training. In the very first rank of his trainers stands *association*. It is his human environment which influences his mind and his feelings, furnishes him his ideals, and sets him on his road and keeps him in it. If he leave that road he will find himself shunned by the people whom he most loves and esteems, and whose approval he most values. He is a chameleon; by the law of his nature he takes the color of his place of resort. The influences about him create his preferences, his aversions, his politics, his tastes, his morals, his religion. He creates none of these things for himself. He *thinks* he does, but that is because he has not examined into the matter. You have seen Presbyterians?

Y. M. Many.

O. M. How did they happen to be Presbyterians and not Congregationalists? And why were the Congregationalists not Baptists, and the Baptists Roman Catholics, and the Roman Catholics Buddhists, and the Buddhists Quakers, and the Quakers Episcopalians, and the Episcopalians Millerites[7] and the Millerites Hindoos, and the Hindoos Atheists and the Atheists Spiritualists, and the Spiritualists Agnostics, and the Agnostics Methodists, and the Methodists Confucians, and the Confucians Unitarians, and the Unitarians Mohammedans, and the Mohammedans Salvation Warriors, and the Salvation Warriors Zoroastrians, and the Zoroastrians Christian Scientists, and the Christian Scientists Mormons—and so on?

Y. M. You may answer your question yourself.

O. M. That list of sects is not a record of *studies*, searchings, seekings after light; it mainly (and sarcastically) indicates what *association* can do. If you know a man's nationality you can come within a split hair of guessing the complexion of his religion: English—Protestant; American—ditto; Spaniard, Frenchman, Irishman, Italian, South American, Austrian— Roman Catholic; Russian—Greek Catholic; Turk—Mohammedan; and so on. And when you know the man's religious complexion, you know what sort of religious books he reads when he wants some more light, and what sort of books he avoids, lest by accident he get more light than he wants. In America if you know which party-collar a voter wears, you know what his associations are, and how he came by his politics, and which breed of newspaper he reads to get light, and which breed he diligently avoids, and which breed of mass-meetings he attends in order to broaden his political knowledge, and which breed of mass-meetings he doesn't attend, except to refute its doctrines with brickbats. We are always hearing of people who are around *seeking after Truth.* I have never seen a (permanent) specimen. I think he has never lived. But I have seen several entirely sincere people who *thought* they were (permanent) Seekers after Truth. They sought diligently, persistently, carefully, cautiously, profoundly, with perfect honesty and nicely adjusted judgment—until they believed that without doubt or question they had found the Truth. *That was the end of the search.* The man spent the rest of his life hunting up shingles wherewith to protect his Truth from the weather. If he was seeking after political Truth he found it in one or another of the hundred political gospels which govern men in the earth; if he was seeking after the Only True Religion he found it in one or another of the three thousand that are on the market. In any case, when he found the Truth *he sought no further*; but from that day forth, with his soldering-iron in one hand and his bludgeon in the other he tinkered its leaks and reasoned with objectors. There have been innumerable Temporary Seekers after Truth—have you ever heard of a permanent one? In the very nature of man such a person is impossible. However, to drop back to the text—training: all training is one form or another of *outside influence*, and *association* is the largest part of it. A man is never anything but what his outside influences have made him. They train him downward or they train him upward—but they *train* him; they are at work upon him all the time.

Y. M. Then if he happen by the accidents of life to be evilly placed there is no help for him, according to your notions—he must train downward.

O. M. No help for him? No help for this chameleon? It is a mistake. It is in his chameleonship that his greatest good fortune lies. He has only to change his habitat—his *associations.* But the impulse to do it must come from the *outside*—he cannot originate it himself, with that purpose in view. Sometimes a very small and accidental thing can furnish him the initiatory impulse and start him on a new road, with a new ideal. The chance remark of a sweetheart, "I hear that you are a coward," may water a seed that shall sprout and bloom and flourish, and end in producing a surprising fruitage—in the fields of war. The history of man is full of such accidents. The accident of a broken leg brought a profane and ribald soldier under religious influences and furnished him a new ideal. From that accident sprang the Order of the Jesuits, and it has been shaking thrones, changing policies, and doing other tremendous work for two hundred years—and will go on.[8] The chance reading of a book or of a paragraph in a newspaper can start a man on a new track and make him renounce his old associations and seek new ones that are *in sympathy with his new ideal*: and the result, for that man, can be an entire change of his way of life.

Y. M. Are you hinting at a scheme of procedure?

O. M. Not a new one—an old one. Old as mankind.

Y. M. What is it?

O. M. Merely the laying of traps for people. Traps baited with *Initiatory Impulses toward high ideals.* It is what the tract-distributer does. It is what the missionary does. It is what governments ought to do.

Y. M. Don't they?

O. M. In one way they do, in another way they don't. They separate the smallpox patients from the healthy people, but in dealing with crime they put the healthy into the pest-house along with the sick. That is to say, they put the beginners in with the confirmed criminals. This would be well if man were naturally inclined to good, but he isn't, and so *association* makes the beginners worse than they were when they went into captivity. It is putting a very severe punishment upon the comparatively innocent at times. They hang a man—which is a trifling punishment; this breaks the hearts of his family—which is a heavy one. They comfortably jail and feed a wife-beater, and leave his innocent wife and children to starve.

Y. M. Do you believe in the doctrine that man is equipped with an intuitive perception of good and evil?

O. M. Adam hadn't it.

Y. M. But has man acquired it since?

O. M. No. I think he has no intuitions of any kind. He gets *all* his ideas, all his impressions, from the outside. I keep repeating this, in the hope that I may so impress it upon you that you will be interested to observe and examine for yourself and see whether, it is true or false.

Y. M. Where did you get your own aggravating notions?

O. M. From the *outside.* I did not invent them. They are gathered from a thousand unknown sources. Mainly *unconsciously* gathered.

Y. M. Don't you believe that God could make an inherently honest man?

O. M. Yes, I know He could. I also know that He never did make one.

Y. M. A wiser observer than you has recorded the fact that "an honest man's the noblest work of God."[9]

O. M. He didn't record a fact, he recorded a falsity. It is windy, and sounds well, but it is not true. God makes a man with honest and dishonest *possibilities* in him and stops there. The man's *associations* develop the possibilities—the one set or the other. The result is accordingly an honest man or a dishonest one.

Y. M. And the honest one is not entitled to—

O. M. Praise? No. How often must I tell you that? *He* is not the architect of his honesty.

Y. M. Now then, I will ask you where there is any sense in training people to lead virtuous lives. What is gained by it?

O. M. The man himself gets large advantages out of it, and that is the main thing—to *him.* He is not a peril to his neighbors, he is not a damage to them—and so *they* get an advantage out of his virtues. That is the main thing to them. It can make this life comparatively comfortable to the parties concerned; the neglect of this training can make this life a constant peril and distress to the parties concerned. That is the main thing to *them.* It can make this life comparatively comfortable to the parties concerned; the *neglect* of this training can make this life a constant peril and distress to the parties concerned.

Y. M. You have said that training is everything; that training is the man *himself*, for it makes him what he is.

O. M. I said training and *another* thing. Let that other thing pass, for the moment. What were you going to say?

Y. M. We have an old servant. She has been with us twenty-two years. Her service used to be faultless, but now she has become very forgetful. We are all fond of her; we all recognize that she cannot help the infirmity which age has brought her; the rest of the family do not scold her for her remissnesses, but at times I do—I can't seem to control myself. Don't I try? I do try. Now, then, when I was ready to dress, this morning, no clean clothes had been put out. I lost my temper; I lose it easiest and quickest in the early morning. I rang; and immediately began to warn myself not to show temper, and to be careful and speak gently. I safeguarded myself most carefully. I even chose the very words I would use: "You've forgotten the clean clothes, Jane." When she appeared in the door I opened my mouth to say that phrase and out of it, moved by an instant surge of passion which I was not expecting and hadn't time to put under control, came the hot rebuke, "You've forgotten them again!" You say a man always does the thing which will best please his Interior Master. Whence came the impulse to make careful preparation to save the girl the humiliation of a rebuke? Did that come from the Master, who is always primarily concerned about *himself*?

O. M. Unquestionably. There is no other source for any impulse. *Secondarily* you made preparation to save the girl, but *primarily* its object was to save yourself, by contenting the Master.

Y. M. How do you mean?

O. M. Has any member of the family ever implored you to watch your temper and not fly out at the girl?

Y. M. Yes. My mother.

O. M. You love her?

Y. M. Oh, more than that!

O. M. You would always do anything in your power to please her?

Y. M. It is a delight to me to do anything to please her!

O. M. Why? *You would do it for pay, solely*—for *profit*. What profit would you expect and certainly receive from the investment?

Y. M. Personally? None. To please *her* is enough.

O. M. It appears, then, that your object, primarily, *wasn't* to save the girl a humiliation, but to *please your mother*. It also appears that to please your mother gives you a strong pleasure. Is not that the profit which you get out of the investment? Isn't that the *real* profit and *first* profit?

Y. M. Oh, well? Go on.

O. M. In *all* transactions, the Interior Master so looks to it that *you get the first profit*. Otherwise there is no transaction.

Y. M. Well, then, if I was so anxious to get that profit and so intent upon it, why did I throw it away by losing my temper?

O. M. In order to get *another* profit which suddenly superseded it in value.

Y. M. Where was it?

O. M. Ambushed behind your born temperament, and waiting for a chance. Your native warm temper suddenly jumped to the front, and *for the moment* its influence was more powerful than your mother's, and abolished it. In that instance you were eager to flash out a hot rebuke and enjoy it. You did enjoy it, didn't you?

Y. M. For—for a quarter of a second. Yes—I did.

O. M. Very well, it is as I have said: the thing which will give you the *most* pleasure, the most satisfaction, in any moment or *fraction* of a moment, is the thing you will always do. You must content the Master's *latest* whim, whatever it may be.

Y. M. But when the tears came into the old servant's eyes I could have cut my hand off for what I had done.

O. M. Right. You had humiliated *yourself*, you see, you had given yourself *pain*. Nothing is of *first* importance to a man except results which damage *him* or profit him—all the rest is *secondary*. Your Master was displeased with you, although you had obeyed him. He required a prompt *repentance*; you obeyed again; you *had* to—there is never any escape from his commands. He is a hard master and fickle; he changes his mind in the fraction of a second, but you must be ready to obey, and you will obey, *always*. If he requires repentance, to content him, you will always furnish it. He must be nursed, petted, coddled, and kept contented, let the terms be what they may.

Y. M. Training! Oh, what is the use of it? Didn't I, and didn't my mother try to train me up to where I would no longer fly out at that girl?

O. M. Have you never managed to keep back a scolding?

Y. M. Oh, certainly—many times.

O. M. More times this year than last?

Y. M. Yes, a good many more.

O. M. More times last year than the year before?

Y. M. Yes.

O. M. There is a large improvement, then, in the two years?

Y. M. Yes, undoubtedly.

O. M. Then your question is answered. You see there is use in training. Keep on. Keep faithfully on. You are doing well.

Y. M. Will my reform reach perfection?

O. M. It will. Up to *your* limit.

Y. M. My limit? What do you mean by that?

O. M. You remember that you said that I said training was *everything.* I corrected you, and said "training and *another* thing." That other thing is *temperament*—that is, the disposition you were born with. *You can't eradicate your disposition nor any rag of it*—you can only put a pressure on it and keep it down and quiet. You have a warm temper?

Y. M. Yes.

O. M. You will never get rid of it; but by watching it you can keep it down nearly all the time. *Its presence is your limit.* Your reform will never quite reach perfection, for your temper will beat you now and then, but you will come near enough. You have made valuable progress and can make more. There *is* use in training. Immense use. Presently you will reach a new stage of development, then your progress will be easier; will proceed on a simpler basis, anyway.

Y. M. Explain.

O. M. You keep back your scoldings now, to please *yourself* by pleasing your *mother*; presently the mere triumphing over your temper will delight your vanity and confer a more delicious pleasure and satisfaction upon you than even the approbation of your mother confers upon you now. You will then labor for yourself directly and at *first hand*, not by the roundabout way through your mother. It simplifies the matter, and it also strengthens the impulse.

Y. M. Ah, dear! But I sha'n't ever reach the point where I will spare the girl for *her* sake *primarily*, not mine?

O. M. Why—yes. In heaven.

Y. M. (*After a reflective pause.*) Temperament. Well, I see one must allow for temperament. It is a large factor, sure enough. My mother is thoughtful, and not hot-tempered. When I was dressed I went to her room; she was not there; I called, she answered from the bathroom. I heard the water running. I inquired. She answered, without temper, that Jane had forgotten her bath, and she was preparing it herself. I offered to ring, but she said, "No, don't do that; it would only distress her to be confronted with her lapse, and would be a rebuke; she doesn't deserve that—she is not to blame for the tricks her memory serves her." I say—has my mother an Interior Master?—and where was he?

O. M. He was there. There, and looking out for his own peace and pleasure and contentment. The girl's distress would have pained *your mother.* Otherwise the girl would have been rung up, distress and all. I know women who would have gotten a No. 1 *pleasure* out of ringing Jane up—and so they would infallibly have pushed the button and obeyed the law of their make and training, which are the servants of their Interior Masters. It is quite likely that a part of your mother's forbearance came from training. The *good* kind of training—whose best and highest function is to see to it that every time it confers a satisfaction upon its pupil a benefit shall fall at second hand upon others.

Y. M. If you were going to condense into an admonition your plan for the general betterment of the race's condition, how would you word it?

### Admonition

O. M. Diligently train your ideals *upward* and *still upward* toward a summit where you will find your chiefest pleasure in conduct which, while contenting you, will be sure to confer benefits upon your neighbor and the community.

Y. M. Is that a new gospel?

O. M. No.

Y. M. It has been taught before?

O. M. For ten thousand years.

Y. M. By whom?

O. M. All the great religions—all the great gospels.

Y. M. Then there is nothing new about it?

O. M. Oh yes, there is. It is candidly stated, this time. That has not been done before.

Y. M. How do you mean?

O. M. Haven't I put *you* first, and your neighbor and the community *afterward*?

Y. M. Well, yes, that is a difference, it is true.

O. M. The difference between straight speaking and crooked; the difference between frankness and shuffling.

Y. M. Explain.

O. M. The others offer you a hundred bribes to be good, thus conceding that the Master inside of you must be conciliated and contented first, and that you will do nothing at *first hand* but for his sake; then they turn square around and require you to do good for *others'* sake *chiefly*; and to do your duty for duty's *sake*, chiefly; and to do acts of *self-sacrifice*. Thus at the outset we all stand upon the same ground—recognition of the supreme and absolute Monarch that resides in man, and we all grovel before him and appeal to him; then those others dodge and shuffle, and face around and unfrankly and inconsistently and illogically change the form of their appeal and direct its persuasions to man's *second-place* powers and to powers which have *no existence* in him, thus advancing them to *first* place; whereas in my Admonition I stick logically and consistently to the original position: I place the Interior Master's requirements *first*, and keep them there.

Y. M. If we grant, for the sake of argument, that your scheme and the other schemes aim at and produce the same result—*right living*—has yours an advantage over the others?

O. M. One, yes—a large one. It has no concealments, no deceptions. When a man leads a right and valuable life under it he is not deceived as to the *real* chief motive which impels him to it—in those other cases he is.

Y. M. Is that an advantage? Is it an advantage to live a lofty life for a mean reason? In the other cases he lives the lofty life under the *impression* that he is living it for a lofty reason. Is not that an advantage?

O. M. Perhaps so. The same advantage he might get out of thinking himself a duke, and living a duke's life and parading in ducal fuss and feathers, when he wasn't a duke at all, and could find it out if he would only examine the herald's records.

Y. M. But anyway, he is obliged to do a duke's part; he puts his hand in his pocket and does his benevolences on as big a scale as he can stand, and that benefits the community.

O. M. He could do that without being a duke.

Y. M. But would he?

O. M. Don't you see where you are arriving?

Y. M. Where?

O. M. At the standpoint of the other schemes: That it is good morals to let an ignorant duke do showy benevolences for his pride's sake, a pretty low motive, and go on doing them unwarned, lest if he were made acquainted with the actual motive which prompted them he might shut up his purse and cease to be good?

Y. M. But isn't it best to leave him in ignorance, as long as he *thinks* he is doing good for others' sake?

O. M. Perhaps so. It is the position of the other schemes. They think humbug is good enough morals when the dividend on it is good deeds and handsome conduct.

Y. M. It is my opinion that under your scheme of a man's doing a good deed for his *own* sake first-off, instead of first for the *good deed's* sake, no man would ever do one.

O. M. Have you committed a benevolence lately?

Y. M. Yes. This morning.

O. M. Give the particulars.

Y. M. The cabin of the old negro woman who used to nurse me when I was a child and who saved my life once at the risk of her own, was burned last night, and she came mourning this morning, and pleading for money to build another one.

O. M. You furnished it?

Y. M. Certainly.

O. M. You were glad you had the money?

Y. M. Money? I hadn't. I sold my horse.

O. M. You were glad you had the horse?

Y. M. Of course I was; for if I hadn't had the horse I should have been incapable, and my *mother* would have captured the chance to set old Sally up.

O. M. You were cordially glad you were not caught out and incapable?

Y. M. Oh, I just was!

O. M. Now, then—

Y. M. Stop where you are! I know your whole catalogue of questions, and I could answer every one of them without your wasting the time to ask them; but I will summarize the whole thing in a single remark: I did the charity knowing it was because the act would give *me* a splendid pleasure, and because old Sally's moving gratitude and delight would give me another one; and because the reflection that she would be happy now and out of her trouble would fill *me* full of happiness. I did the whole thing with my eyes open and recognizing and realizing that I was looking out for *my* share of the profits *first*. Now then, I have confessed. Go on.

O. M. I haven't anything to offer; you have covered the whole ground. Could you have been any *more* strongly moved to help Sally out of her trouble—could you have done the deed any more eagerly—if you had been under the delusion that you were doing it for *her* sake and profit only?

Y. M. No! Nothing in the world could have made the impulse which moved me more powerful, more masterful, more thoroughly irresistible. I played the limit!

O. M. Very well. You begin to suspect—and I claim to *know*—that when a man is a shade *more strongly moved* to do *one* of two things or of two dozen things than he is to do any one of the *others*, he will infallibly do that *one* thing, be it good or be it evil; and if it be good, not all the beguilements of all the casuistries can increase the strength of the impulse by a single shade or add a shade to the comfort and contentment he will get out of the act.

Y. M. Then you believe that such tendency toward doing good as is in men's hearts would not be diminished by the removal of the delusion that good deeds are done primarily for the sake of No. 2 instead of for the sake of No. 1?

O. M. That is what I fully believe.

Y. M. Doesn't it somehow seem to take from the dignity of the deed?

O. M. If there is dignity in falsity, it does. It removes that.

Y. M. What is left for the moralist to do?

O. M. Teach unreservedly what he already teaches with one side of his mouth and takes back with the other: Do right *for your own sake,* and be happy in knowing that your *neighbor* will certainly share in the benefits resulting.

Y. M. Repeat your Admonition.

O. M. *Diligently train your ideals upward and still upward toward a summit where you will find your chiefest pleasure in conduct which, while contenting you, will be sure to confer benefits upon your neighbor and the community.*

Y. M. One's every act proceeds from *exterior influences,* you think?

O. M. Yes.

Y. M. If I conclude to rob a person, I am not the *originator* of the idea, but it comes in from the *outside?* I see him handling money—for instance—and *that* moves me to the crime?

O. M. That, by itself? Oh, certainly not. It is merely the *latest* outside influence of a procession of preparatory influences stretching back over a period of years. No *single* outside influence can make a man do a thing which is at war with his training. The most it can do is to start his mind on a new tract and open it to the reception of *new* influences—as in the case of Ignatius Loyola. In time these influences can train him to a point where it will be consonant with his new character to yield to the *final* influence and do that thing. I will put the case in a form which will make my theory clear to you, I think. Here are two ingots of virgin gold. They shall represent a couple of characters which have been refined and perfected in the virtues by years of diligent right training. Suppose you wanted to break down these strong and well-compacted characters—what influence would you bring to bear upon the ingots?

Y. M. Work it out yourself. Proceed.

O. M. Suppose I turn upon one of them a steam-jet during a long succession of hours. Will there be a result?

Y. M. None that I know of.

O. M. Why?

Y. M. A steam-jet cannot break down such a substance.

O. M. Very well. The steam is an *outside influence*, but it is ineffective because the gold *takes no interest in it*. The ingot remains as it was. Suppose we add to the steam some quicksilver in a vaporized condition, and turn the jet upon the ingot, will there be an instantaneous result?

Y. M. No.

O. M. The *quicksilver* is an outside influence which gold (by its peculiar nature—say *temperament, disposition*) *cannot be indifferent to*. It stirs the interest of the gold, although we do not perceive it; but a *single* application of the influence works no damage. Let us continue the application in a steady stream, and call each minute a year. By the end of ten or twenty minutes—ten or twenty years—the little ingot is sodden with quicksilver, its virtues are gone, its character is degraded. At last it is ready to yield to a temptation which it would have taken no notice of, ten or twenty years ago. We will apply that temptation in the form of a pressure of my finger. You note the result?

Y. M. Yes; the ingot has crumbled to sand. I understand, now. It is not the *single* outside influence that does the work, but only the *last* one of a long and disintegrating accumulation of them. I see, now, how my *single* impulse to rob the man is not the one that makes me do it, but only the *last* one of a preparatory series. You might illustrate it with a parable.

## A Parable

O. M. I will. There was once a pair of New England boys—twins. They were alike in good dispositions, fleckless morals, and personal appearance. They were the models of the Sunday-school. At fifteen George had an opportunity to go as cabin-boy in a whale-ship, and sailed away for the Pacific. Henry remained at home in the village. At eighteen George was a sailor before the mast, and Henry was teacher of the advanced Bible class. At twenty-two George, through fighting-habits and drinking-habits acquired at sea and in the sailor boarding-houses of the European and Oriental ports, was a common rough in Hong-Kong, and out of a job; and Henry was superintendent of the Sunday-school. At twenty-six George was a wanderer, a tramp, and Henry was pastor of the village church. Then George came home, and was Henry's guest. One evening a man passed by and turned down the lane, and Henry said, with a pathetic smile, "Without intending me a discomfort, that man is always keeping me reminded of my pinching poverty, for he carries heaps of money about him, and goes by here every evening of his life." That *outside influence*—that remark—was enough for George, but *it* was not the one that made him ambush the man and rob him, it merely represented the eleven years' accumulation of such influences, and gave birth to the act for which their long gestation had made preparation. It had never entered the head of Henry to rob the man—his ingot had been subjected to clean steam only; but George's had been subjected to vaporized quicksilver.

# V
## MORE ABOUT THE MACHINE

Note.—When Mrs. W. asks how can a millionaire give a single dollar to colleges and museums while one human being is destitute of bread, she has answered her question herself. Her feeling for the poor shows that she has a standard of benevolence; therefore she has conceded the millionaire's privilege of having a standard; since she evidently requires him to adopt her standard, she is by that act requiring herself to adopt his. The human being always looks down when he is examining another person's standard; he never finds one that he has to examine by looking up.

### The Man-Machine Again

YOUNG MAN. You really think man is a mere machine?

OLD MAN. I do.

Y. M. And that his mind works automatically and is independent of his control—carries on thought on its own hook?

O. M. Yes. It is diligently at work, unceasingly at work, during every waking moment. Have you never tossed about all night, imploring, beseeching, commanding your mind to stop work and let you go to sleep?—you who perhaps imagine that your mind is your servant and must obey your orders, think what you tell it to think, and stop when you tell it to stop. When it chooses to work, there is no way to keep it still for an instant. The brightest man would not be able to supply it with subjects if he had to hunt them up. If it needed the man's help it would wait for him to give it work when he wakes in the morning.

Y. M. Maybe it does.

O. M. No, it begins right away, before the man gets wide enough awake to give it a suggestion. He may go to sleep saying, "The moment I wake I will think upon such and such a subject," but he will fail. His mind will be too quick for him; by the time he has become nearly enough awake to be half conscious, he will find that it is already at work upon another subject. Make the experiment and see.

Y. M. At any rate, he can make it stick to a subject if he wants to.

O. M. Not if it finds another that suits it better. As a rule it will listen to neither a dull speaker nor a bright one. It refuses all persuasion. The dull speaker wearies it and sends it far away in idle dreams; the bright speaker throws out stimulating ideas which it goes chasing after and is at once unconscious of him and his talk. You cannot keep your mind from wandering, if it wants to; it is master, not you.

### After an Interval of Days

O. M. Now, dreams—but we will examine that later. Meantime, did you try commanding your mind to wait for orders from you, and not do any thinking on its own hook?

Y. M. Yes, I commanded it to stand ready to take orders when I should wake in the morning.

O. M. Did it obey?

Y. M. No. It went to thinking of something of its own initiation, without waiting for me. Also—as you suggested—at night I appointed a theme for it to begin on in the morning, and commanded it to begin on that one and no other.

O. M. Did it obey?

Y. M. No.

O. M. How many times did you try the experiment?

Y. M. Ten.

O. M. How many successes did you score?

Y. M. Not one.

O. M. It is as I have said: the mind is independent of the man. He has no control over it; it does as it pleases. It will take up a subject in spite of him; it will stick to it in spite of him; it will throw it aside in spite of him. It is entirely independent of him.

Y. M. Go on. Illustrate.

O. M. Do you know chess?

Y. M. I learned it a week ago.

O. M. Did your mind go on playing the game all night that first night?

Y. M. Don't mention it!

O. M. It was eagerly, unsatisfiably interested; it rioted in the combinations; you implored it to drop the game and let you get some sleep?

Y. M. Yes. It wouldn't listen; it played right along. It wore me out and I got up haggard and wretched in the morning.

O. M. At some time or other you have been captivated by a ridiculous rhyme-jingle?

Y. M. Indeed, yes!

> "I saw Esau kissing Kate,
>    And she saw I saw Esau;
> I saw Esau, he saw Kate,
>    And she saw—"

And so on. My mind went mad with joy over it. It repeated it all day and all night for a week in spite of all I could do to stop it, and it seemed to me that I must surely go crazy.

O. M. And the new popular song?

Y. M. Oh yes! "In the Swee-eet By and By";[10] etc. Yes, the new popular song with the taking melody sings through one's head day and night, asleep and awake, till one is a wreck. There is no getting the mind to let it alone.

O. M. Yes, asleep as well as awake. The mind is quite independent. It is master. You have nothing to do with it. It is so apart from you that it can conduct its affairs, sing its songs, play its chess, weave its complex and ingeniously constructed dreams, while you sleep. It has no use for your help, no use for your guidance, and never uses either, whether you be asleep or awake. You have imagined that you could originate a thought in your mind, and you have sincerely believed you could do it.

Y. M. Yes, I have had that idea.

O. M. Yet you can't originate a dream-thought for it to work out, and get it accepted?

Y. M. No.

O. M. And you can't dictate its procedure after it has originated a dream-thought for itself?

Y. M. No. No one can do it. Do you think the waking mind and the dream mind are the same machine?

O. M. There is argument for it. We have wild and fantastic day-thoughts? Things that are dream-like?

Y. M. Yes—like Mr. Wells's man who invented a drug that made him invisible;[11] and like the Arabian of the Thousand Nights.

O. M. And there are dreams that are rational, simple, consistent, and unfantastic?

Y. M. Yes. I have dreams that are like that. Dreams that are just like real life; dreams in which there are several persons with distinctly differentiated characters—inventions of my mind and yet strangers to me: a vulgar person; a refined one; a wise person; a fool; a cruel person; a kind and compassionate one; a quarrelsome person; a peacemaker; old persons and young; beautiful girls and homely ones. They talk in character, each preserves his own characteristics. There are vivid fights, vivid and biting insults, vivid love-passages; there are tragedies and comedies, there are griefs that go to one's heart, there are sayings and doings that make you laugh: indeed, the whole thing is exactly like real life.

O. M. Your dreaming mind originates the scheme, consistently and artistically develops it, and carries the little drama creditably through—all without help or suggestion from you?

Y. M. Yes.

O. M. It is argument that it could do the like awake without help or suggestion from you—and I think it does. It is argument that it is the same old mind in both cases, and never needs your help. I think the mind is purely a machine, a thoroughly independent machine, an automatic machine. Have you tried the other experiment which I suggested to you?

Y. M. Which one?

O. M. The one which was to determine how much influence you have over your mind—if any.

Y. M. Yes, and got more or less entertainment out of it. I did as you ordered: I placed two texts before my eyes—one a dull one and barren of interest, the other one full of interest, inflamed with it, white-hot with it. I commanded my mind to busy itself solely with the dull one.

O. M. Did it obey?

Y. M. Well, no, it didn't. It busied itself with the other one.

O. M. Did you try hard to make it obey?

Y. M. Yes, I did my honest best.

O. M. What was the text which it refused to be interested in or think about?

Y. M. It was this question: If A owes B a dollar and a half, and B owes C two and three-quarters, and C owes A thirty-five cents, and D and A together owe E and B three-sixteenths of—of—I don't remember the rest, now, but anyway it was wholly uninteresting, and I could not force my mind to stick to it even half a minute at a time; it kept flying off to the other text.

O. M. What was the other text?

Y. M. It is no matter about that.

O. M. But what was it?

Y. M. A photograph.

O. M. Your own?

Y. M. No. It was hers.

O. M. You really made an honest good test. Did you make a second trial?

Y. M. Yes. I commanded my mind to interest itself in the morning paper's report of the pork-market, and at the same time I reminded it of an experience of mine of sixteen years ago. It refused to consider the pork and gave its whole blazing interest to that ancient incident.

O. M. What was the incident?

Y. M. An armed desperado slapped my face in the presence of twenty spectators. It makes me wild and murderous every time I think of it.

O. M. Good tests, both; very good tests. Did you try my other suggestion?

Y. M. The one which was to prove to me that if I would leave my mind to its own devices it would find things to think about without any of my help, and thus convince me that it was a machine, an automatic machine, set in motion by exterior influences, and as independent of me as it could be if it were in some one else's skull? Is that the one?

O. M. Yes.

Y. M. I tried it. I was shaving. I had slept well, and my mind was very lively, even gay and frisky. It was reveling in a fantastic and joyful episode of my remote boyhood which had suddenly flashed up in my memory—moved to this by the spectacle of a yellow cat picking its way carefully along the top of the garden wall. The color of this cat brought the bygone cat before me, and I saw her walking along the side-step of the pulpit; saw her walk on to a large sheet of sticky fly-paper and get all her feet involved; saw her struggle and fall down, helpless and dissatisfied, more and more urgent, more and more unreconciled, more and more mutely profane; saw the silent congregation quivering like jelly, and the tears running down their faces. I saw it all. The sight of the tears whisked my mind to a far distant and a sadder scene—in Terra del Fuego—and with Darwin's eyes I saw a naked great savage hurl his little boy against the rocks for a trifling fault; saw the poor mother gather up her dying child and hug it to her breast and weep, uttering no word. Did my mind stop to mourn with that nude black sister of mine? No—it was far away from that scene in an instant, and was busying itself with an ever-recurring and disagreeable dream of mine. In this dream I always find myself, stripped to my shirt, cringing and dodging about in the midst of a great drawing-room throng of finely dressed ladies and gentlemen, and wondering how I got there. And so on and so on, picture after picture, incident after incident, a drifting panorama of ever-changing, ever-dissolving views manufactured by my mind without any help from me—why, it would take me two hours to merely name the multitude of things my mind tallied off and photographed in fifteen minutes, let alone describe them to you.

O. M. A man's mind, left free, has no use for his help. But there is one way whereby he can get its help when he desires it.

Y. M. What is that way?

O. M. When your mind is racing along from subject to subject and strikes an inspiring one, open your mouth and begin talking upon that matter—or take your pen and use that. It will interest your mind and concentrate it, and it will pursue the subject with satisfaction. It will take full charge, and furnish the words itself.

Y. M. But don't I tell it what to say?

O. M. There are certainty occasions when you haven't time. The words leap out before you know what is coming.

Y. M. For instance?

O. M. Well, take a "flash of wit"—repartee. Flash is the right word. It is out instantly. There is no time to arrange the words. There is no thinking, no reflecting. Where there is a witmechanism it is automatic in its action and needs no help. Where the wit-mechanism is lacking, no amount of study and reflection can manufacture the product.

Y. M. You really think a man originates nothing, creates nothing.

### The Thinking-Process

O. M. I do. Men perceive, and their brain-machines automatically combine the things perceived. That is all.

Y. M. The steam-engine?

O. M. It takes fifty men a hundred years to invent it. One meaning of invent is discover. I use the word in that sense. Little by little they discover and apply the multitude of details that go to make the perfect engine. Watt noticed that confined steam was strong enough to lift the lid of the teapot.[12] He didn't create the idea, he merely discovered the fact; the cat had noticed it a hundred times. From the teapot he evolved the cylinder—from the displaced lid he evolved the piston-rod. To attach something to the piston-rod to be moved by it, was a simple matter—crank and wheel. And so there was a working engine.[13]

One by one, improvements were discovered by men who used their eyes, not their creating powers—for they hadn't any—and now, after a hundred years the patient contributions of fifty or a hundred observers stand compacted in the wonderful machine which drives the ocean liner.

Y. M. A Shakespearian play?

O. M. The process is the same. The first actor was a savage. He reproduced in his theatrical war-dances, scalp-dances, and so on, incidents which he had seen in real life. A more advanced civilization produced more incidents, more episodes; the actor and the story-teller borrowed them. And so the drama grew, little by little, stage by stage. It is made up of the facts of life, not creations. It took centuries to develop the Greek drama. It borrowed from preceding ages; it lent to the ages that came after. Men observe and combine, that is all. So does a rat.

Y. M. How?

O. M. He observes a smell, he infers a cheese, he seeks and finds. The astronomer observes this and that; adds his this and that to the this-and-thats of a hundred predecessors, infers an invisible planet, seeks it and finds it. The rat gets into a trap; gets out with trouble; infers that cheese in traps lacks value, and meddles with that trap no more. The astronomer is very proud of his achievement, the rat is proud of his. Yet both are machines; they have done machine work, they have originated nothing, they have no right to be vain; the whole credit belongs to their Maker. They are entitled to no honors, no praises, no monuments when they die, no remembrance. One is a complex and elaborate machine, the other a simple and limited machine, but they are alike in principle, function, and process, and neither of them works otherwise than automatically, and neither of them may righteously claim a *personal* superiority or a personal dignity above the other.

Y. M. In earned personal dignity, then, and in personal merit for what he does, it follows of necessity that he is on the same level as a rat?

O. M. His brother the rat; yes, that is how it seems to me. Neither of them being entitled to any personal merit for what he does, it follows of necessity that neither of them has a right to arrogate to himself (personally created) superiorities over his brother.

Y. M. Are you determined to go on believing in these insanities? Would you go on believing in them in the face of able arguments backed by collated facts and instances?

O. M. I have been a humble, earnest, and sincere Truth-Seeker.

Y. M. Very well?

O. M. The humble, earnest, and sincere Truth-Seeker is always convertible by such means.

Y. M. I am thankful to God to hear you say this, for now I know that your conversion—

O. M. Wait. You misunderstand. I said I have *been* a Truth-Seeker.

Y. M. Well?

O. M. I am not that now. Have you forgotten? I told you that there are none but temporary Truth-Seekers; that a permanent one is a human impossibility; that as soon as the Seeker finds what he is thoroughly convinced is the Truth, he seeks no further, but gives the rest of his days to hunting junk to patch it and caulk it and prop it with, and make it weather-proof and keep it from caving in on him. Hence the Presbyterian remains a Presbyterian, the Mohammedan a Mohammedan, the Spiritualist a Spiritualist, the Democrat a Democrat, the Republican a Republican, the Monarchist a Monarchist; and if a humble, earnest, and sincere Seeker after Truth should find it in the proposition that the moon is made of green cheese nothing could ever budge him from that position; for he is nothing but an automatic machine, and must obey the laws of his construction.

Y. M. And so—

O. M. Having found the Truth; perceiving that beyond question man has but one moving impulse—the contenting of his own spirit—and is merely a machine and entitled to no personal merit for anything he does, it is not humanly possible for me to seek further. The rest of my days will be spent in patching and painting and puttying and caulking my priceless possession and in looking the other way when an imploring argument or a damaging fact approaches.

# VI

## Instinct and Thought

YOUNG MAN. It is odious. Those drunken theories of yours, advanced a while ago—concerning the rat and all that—strip Man bare of all his dignities, grandeurs, sublimities.

OLD MAN. He hasn't any to strip—they are shams, stolen clothes. He claims credits which belong solely to his Maker.

Y. M. But you have no right to put him on a level with a rat.

O. M. I don't—morally. That would not be fair to the rat. The rat is well above him, there.

Y. M. Are you joking?

O. M. No, I am not.

Y. M. Then what do you mean?

O. M. That comes under the head of the Moral Sense. It is a large question. Let us finish with what we are about now, before we take it up.

Y. M. Very well. You have seemed to concede that you place Man and the rat on a level. What is it? The intellectual?

O. M. In form—not in degree.

Y. M. Explain.

O. M. I think that the rat's mind and the man's mind are the same machine, but of unequal capacities—like yours and Edison's; like the African pygmy's and Homer's; like the Bushman's and Bismarck's.

Y. M. How are you going to make that out, when the lower animals have no mental quality but instinct, while man possesses reason?

O. M. What is instinct?

Y. M. It is merely unthinking and mechanical exercise of inherited habit.

O. M. What originated the habit?

Y. M. The first animal started it, its descendants have inherited it.

O. M. How did the first one come to start it?

Y. M. I don't know; but it didn't *think* it out.

O. M. How do you know it didn't?

Y. M. Well—I have a right to suppose it didn't, anyway.

O. M. I don't believe you have. What is thought?

Y. M. I know what you call it: the mechanical and automatic putting together of impressions received from outside, and drawing an inference from them.

O. M. Very good. Now my idea of the meaningless term "instinct" is, that it is merely *petrified thought*; solidified and made inanimate by habit; thought which was once alive and awake, but is become unconscious— walks in its sleep, so to speak.

Y. M. Illustrate it.

O. M. Take a herd of cows, feeding in a pasture. Their heads are all turned in one direction. They do that instinctively; they gain nothing by it, they have no reason for it, they don't know why they do it. It is an inherited habit which was originally thought—that is to say, observation of an exterior fact, and a valuable inference drawn from that observation and confirmed by experience. The original wild ox noticed that with the wind in his favor he could smell his enemy in time to escape; then he inferred that it was worth while to keep his nose to the wind. That is the process which man calls reasoning. Man's thought-machine works just like the other animals', but it is a better one and more Edisonian. Man, in the ox's place, would go further, reason wider: he would face part of the herd the other way and protect both front and rear.

Y. M. Did you say the term instinct is meaningless?

O. M. I think it is a bastard word. I think it confuses us; for as a rule it applies itself to habits and impulses which had a far-off origin in thought, and now and then breaks the rule and applies itself to habits which can hardly claim a thought-origin.

Y. M. Give an instance.

O. M. Well, in putting on trousers a man always inserts the same old leg first—never the other one. There is no advantage in that, and no sense in it. All men do it, yet no man thought it out and adopted it of set purpose, I imagine. But it is a habit which is transmitted, no doubt, and will continue to be transmitted.

Y. M. Can you prove that the habit exists?

O. M. You can prove it, if you doubt. If you will take a man to a clothing-store and watch him try on a dozen pairs of trousers, you will see.

Y. M. The cow illustration is not—

O. M. Sufficient to show that a dumb animal's mental machine is just the same as a man's and its reasoning processes the same? I will illustrate further. If you should hand Mr. Edison a box which you caused to fly open by some concealed device he would infer a spring, and would hunt for it and find it. Now an uncle of mine had an old horse who used to get into the closed lot where the corn-crib was and dishonestly take the corn. I got the punishment myself, as it was supposed that I had heedlessly failed to insert the wooden pin which kept the gate closed. These persistent punishments fatigued me; they also caused me to infer the existence of a culprit, somewhere; so I hid myself and watched the gate. Presently the horse came and pulled the pin out with his teeth and went in. Nobody taught him that; he had observed—then thought it out for himself. His process did not differ from Edison's; he put this and that together and drew an inference—and the peg, too; but I made him sweat for it.

Y. M. It has something of the seeming of thought about it. Still it is not very elaborate. Enlarge.

O. M. Suppose that Edison has been enjoying some one's hospitalities. He comes again by and by, and the house is vacant. He infers that his host has moved. A while afterward, in another town, he sees the man enter a house; he infers that that is the new home, and follows to inquire. Here, now, is the experience of a gull, as related by a naturalist. The scene is a Scotch fishing village where the gulls were kindly treated. This particular gull visited a cottage; was fed; came next day and was fed again; came into the house, next time, and ate with the family; kept on doing this almost daily, thereafter. But, once the gull was away on a journey for a few days, and when it returned the house was vacant. Its friends had removed to a village three miles distant. Several months later it saw the head of the family on the street there, followed him home, entered the house without excuse or apology, and became a daily guest again. Gulls do not rank high mentally, but this one had memory and the reasoning faculty, you see, and applied them Edisonially.

Y. M. Yet it was not an Edison and couldn't be developed into one.

O. M. Perhaps not. Could you?

Y. M. That is neither here nor there. Go on.

O. M. If Edison were in trouble and a stranger helped him out of it and next day he got into the same difficulty again, he would infer the wise thing to do in case he knew the stranger's address. Here is a case of a bird and a stranger as related by a naturalist. An Englishman saw a bird flying around about his dog's head, down in the grounds, and uttering cries of distress. He went there to see about it. The dog had a young bird in his mouth—unhurt. The gentleman rescued it and put it on a bush and brought the dog away. Early the next morning the mother bird came for the gentleman, who was sitting on his veranda, and by its manoeuvers persuaded him to follow it to a distant part of the grounds—flying a little way in front of him and waiting for him to catch up, and so on; and keeping to the winding path, too, instead of flying the near way across lots. The distance covered was four hundred yards. The same dog was the culprit; he had the young bird and once more he had to give it up. Now the mother bird had reasoned it all out: since the stranger had helped her once, she inferred that he would do it again; she know where to find him, and she went upon her errand with confidence. Her mental processes were what Edison's would have been. She put this and that together—and that is all that thought *is*—and out of them built her logical arrangement of inferences. Edison couldn't have done it any better himself.

Y. M. Do you believe that many of the dumb animals can think?

O. M. Yes—the elephant, the monkey, the horse, the dog, the parrot, the macaw, the mocking-bird, and many others. The elephant whose mate fell into a pit, and who dumped dirt and rubbish into the pit till the bottom was raised high enough to enable the captive to step out, was equipped with the reasoning quality. I conceive that all animals that can learn things through teaching and drilling have to know how to observe, and put this and that together and draw an inference—the process of thinking. Could you teach an idiot the manual of arms, and to advance, retreat, and go through complex field manoeuvers at the word of command?

Y. M. Not if he were a thorough idiot.

O. M. Well, canary-birds can learn all that; dogs and elephants learn all sorts of wonderful things. They must surely be able to notice, and to put things together, and say to themselves, "I get the idea, now: when I do so and so, as per order, I am praised and fed; when I do differently I am punished." Fleas can be taught nearly anything that a Congressman can.

Y. M. Granting, then, that dumb animals are able to think upon a low plane, is there any that can think upon a high one? Is there one that is well up toward man?

O. M. Yes. As a thinker and planner the ant is the equal of any savage race of men; as a self-educated specialist in several arts she is the superior of any savage race of men; and in one or two high mental qualities she is above the reach of any man, savage or civilized!

Y. M. Oh, come! you are abolishing the intellectual frontier which separates man and beast.

O. M. I beg your pardon. One cannot abolish what does not exist.

Y. M. You are not in earnest, I hope. You cannot mean to seriously say there is no such frontier.

O. M. I do say it seriously. The instances of the horse, the gull, the mother bird, and the elephant show that those creatures put their this's and thats together just as Edison would have done it and drew the same inferences that he would have drawn. Their mental machinery was just like his, also its manner of working. Their equipment was as inferior to his in elaboration as a Waterbury is inferior to the Strasburg clock,[14] but that is the only difference—there is no frontier.

Y. M. It looks exasperatingly true; and is distinctly offensive. It elevates the dumb beasts to—

O. M. Let us drop that lying phrase, and call them the Unrevealed Creatures; so far as we can know, there is no such thing as a dumb beast.

Y. M. On what grounds do you make that assertion?

O. M. On quite simple ones. "Dumb" beast suggests an animal that has no thought-machinery, no understanding, no speech, no way of communicating what is in its mind. We know that a hen has speech. We cannot understand everything she says, but we easily learn two or three of her phrases. We know when she is saying, "I have laid an egg"; we know when she is saying to the chicks, "Run here, dears, I've found a worm"; we know what she is saying when she voices a warning: "Quick! hurry! gather yourselves under mamma, there's a hawk coming!" We understand the cat when she stretches herself out, purring with affection and contentment and lifts up a soft voice and says, "Come, kitties, supper's ready"; we understand her when she goes mourning about and says, "Where can they be? They are lost. Won't you help me hunt for them?" and we understand the disreputable Tom when he challenges at midnight from his shed, "You come over here, you product of immoral commerce, and I'll make your fur fly!" We understand a few of a dog's phrases and we learn to understand a few of the remarks and gestures of any bird or other animal that we domesticate and observe. The clearness and exactness of the few of the hen's speeches which we understand is argument that she can communicate to her kind a hundred things which we cannot comprehend—in a word, that she can converse. And this argument is also applicable in the case of others of the great army of the Unrevealed. It is just like man's vanity and impertinence to call an animal dumb because it is dumb to his dull perceptions. Now as to the ant—

Y. M. Yes, go back to the ant, the creature that—as you seem to think—sweeps away the last vestige of an intellectual frontier between man and the Unrevealed.

O. M. That is what she surely does. In all his history the aboriginal Australian never thought out a house for himself and built it. The ant is an amazing architect. She is a wee little creature, but she builds a strong and enduring house eight feet high—a house which is as large in proportion to her size as is the largest capitol or cathedral in the world compared to man's size. No savage race has produced architects who could approach the ant in genius or culture. No civilized race has produced architects who could plan a house better for the uses proposed than can hers. Her house contains a throne-room; nurseries for her young; granaries; apartments for her soldiers, her workers, etc.; and they and the multifarious halls and corridors which communicate with them are arranged and distributed with an educated and experienced eye for convenience and adaptability.

Y. M. That could be mere instinct.

O. M. It would elevate the savage if he had it. But let us look further before we decide. The ant has soldiers—battalions, regiments, armies; and they have their appointed captains and generals, who lead them to battle.

Y. M. That could be instinct, too.

O. M. We will look still further. The ant has a system of government; it is well planned, elaborate, and is well carried on.

Y. M. Instinct again.

O. M. She has crowds of slaves, and is a hard and unjust employer of forced labor.

Y. M. Instinct.

O. M. She has cows, and milks them.

Y. M. Instinct, of course.

O. M. In Texas she lays out a farm twelve feet square, plants it, weeds it, cultivates it, gathers the crop and stores it away.

Y. M. Instinct, all the same.

O. M. The ant discriminates between friend and stranger. Sir John Lubbock took ants from two different nests, made them drunk with whisky and laid them, unconscious, by one of the nests, near some water. Ants from the nest came and examined and discussed these disgraced creatures, then carried their friends home and threw the strangers overboard. Sir John repeated the experiment a number of times. For a time the sober ants did as they had done at first—carried their friends home and threw the strangers overboard. But finally they lost patience, seeing that their reformatory efforts went for nothing, and threw both friends and strangers overboard.[15] Come—is this instinct, or is it thoughtful and intelligent discussion of a thing new—absolutely new—to their experience; with a verdict arrived at, sentence passed, and judgment executed? Is it instinct?—thought petrified by ages of habit—or isn't it brand-new thought, inspired by the new occasion, the new circumstances?

Y. M. I have to concede it. It was not a result of habit; it has all the look of reflection, thought, putting this and that together, as you phrase it. I believe it was thought.

O. M. I will give you another instance of thought. Franklin had a cup of sugar on a table in his room. The ants got at it. He tried several preventives; the ants rose superior to them. Finally he contrived one which shut off access—probably set the table's legs in pans of water, or drew a circle of tar around the cup, I don't remember. At any rate, he watched to see what they would do. They tried various schemes—failures, every one. The ants were badly puzzled. Finally they held a consultation, discussed the problem, arrived at a decision—and this time they beat that great philosopher. They formed in procession, crossed the floor, climbed the wall, marched across the ceiling to a point just over the cup, then one by one they let go and fell down into it! Was that instinct—thought petrified by ages of inherited habit?

Y. M. No, I don't believe it was. I believe it was a newly reasoned scheme to meet a new emergency.

O. M. Very well. You have conceded the reasoning power in two instances. I come now to a mental detail wherein the ant is a long way the superior of any human being. Sir John Lubbock proved by many experiments that an ant knows a stranger ant of her own species in a moment, even when the stranger is disguised—with paint. Also he proved that an ant knows every individual in her hive of five hundred thousand souls. Also, after a year's absence of one of the five hundred thousand she will straightway recognize the returned absentee and grace the recognition with an affectionate welcome. How are these recognitions made? Not by color, for painted ants were recognized. Not by smell, for ants that had been dipped in chloroform were recognized. Not by speech and not by antennæ signs nor contacts, for the drunken and motionless ants were recognized and the friend discriminated from the stranger. The ants were all of the same species, therefore the friends had to be recognized by form and feature—friends who formed part of a hive of hundred thousand! Has any man a memory for form and feature approaching that?

Y. M. Certainly not.

O. M. Franklin's ants and Lubbock's ants show fine capacities of putting this and that together in new and untried emergencies and deducting smart the combinations—a man's mental process exactly. With memory to help, man preserves his observations and reasonings, reflects upon them, adds to them, recombines, and so proceeds, stage by stage, to far results—from the teakettle to the ocean greyhound's complex engine; from personal labor to slave labor; from wigwam to palace; from the capricious chase to agriculture and stored food; from nomadic life to stable government and concentrated authority; from incoherent hordes to massed armies. The ant has observation, the reasoning faculty, and the preserving adjunct of a prodigious memory; she has duplicated man's development and the essential features of his civilization, and you call it all instinct!

Y. M. Perhaps I lacked the reasoning faculty myself.

O. M. Well, don't tell anybody, and don't do it again.

Y. M. We have come a good way. As a result—as I understand it—I am required to concede that there is absolutely no intellectual frontier separating Man and the Unrevealed Creatures?

O. M. That is what you are required to concede. There is no such frontier—there is no way to get around that. Man has a finer and more capable machine in him than those others, but it is the same machine and works in the same way. And neither he nor those others can command the machine—it is strictly automatic, independent of control, works when it pleases, and when it doesn't please, it can't be forced.

Y. M. Then man and the other animals are all alike, as to mental machinery, and there isn't any difference of any stupendous magnitude between them, except in quality, not in kind.

O. M. That is about the state of it—intellectually. There are pronounced limitations on both sides. We can't learn to understand much of their language, but the dog, the elephant, etc., learn to understand a very great deal of ours. To that extent they are our superiors. On the other hand, they can't learn reading, writing, etc., nor any of our fine and high things, and there we have a large advantage over them.

Y. M. Very well, let them have what they've got, and welcome; there is still a wall, and a lofty one. They haven't got the Moral Sense; we have it, and it lifts us immeasurably above them.

O. M. What makes you think that?

Y. M. Now look here—let us call a halt. I have stood the other infamies and insanities and that is enough; I am not going to have man and the other aniinals put on the same level morally.

O. M. I wasn't going to hoist man up to that.

Y. M. This is too much! I think it is not right to jest about such things.

O. M. I am not jesting, I am merely reflecting a plain and simple truth—and without uncharitableness. The fact that man knows right from wrong proves his *intellectual* superiority to the other creatures; but the fact that he can *do* wrong proves his *moral* inferiority to any creature that *cannot.* It is my belief that this position is not assailable.

### Free Will

Y. M. What is your opinion regarding Free Will?

O. M. That there is no such thing. Did the man possess it who gave the old woman his last shilling and trudged home in the storm?

Y. M. He had the choice between succoring the old woman and leaving her to suffer. Isn't it so?

O. M. Yes, there was a choice to be made, between bodily comfort on the one hand and the comfort of the spirit on the other. The body made a strong appeal, of course—the body would be quite sure to do that; the spirit made a counter appeal. A choice had to be made between the two appeals, and was made. Who or what determined that choice?

Y. M. Any one but you would say that the man determined it, and that in doing it he exercised Free Will.

O. M. We are constantly assured that every man is endowed with Free Will, and that he can and must exercise it where he is offered a choice between good conduct and less-good conduct. Yet we clearly saw that in that man's case he really had no Free Will: his temperament, his training, and the daily influences which had molded him and made him what he was, *compelled* him to rescue the old woman and thus save *himself*—save himself from spiritual pain, from unendurable wretchedness. He did not make the choice, it was made *for* him by forces which he could not control. Free Will has always existed in *words*, but it stops there, I think— stops short of *fact*. I would not use those words—Free Will—but others.

Y. M. What others?

O. M. Free Choice.

Y. M. What is the difference?

O. M. The one implies untrammeled power to act as you please, the other implies nothing beyond a mere *mental process*: the critical ability to determine which of two things is nearest right and just.

Y. M. Make the differonce clear, please.

O. M. The mind can freely *select, choose, point out* the right and just one—its function stops there. It can go no further in the matter. It has no authority to say that the right one shall be acted upon and the wrong one discarded. That authority is in other hands.

Y. M. The man's?

O. M. In the machine which stands for him. In his born disposition and the character which has been built around it by training and environment.

Y. M. It will act upon the right one of the two?

O. M. It will do as it pleases in the matter. George Washington's machine would act upon the right one; Pizarro's mind would know which was the right one and which the wrong, but the Master inside of Pizarro would act upon the wrong one.[16]

Y. M. Then as I understand it a bad man's mental machinery calmly and judicially points out which of two things is right and just—

O. M. Yes, and his *moral* machinery will freely act upon the one or the other, according to its make, and be quite indifferent to the *mind's* feelings concerning the matter—that is, *would* be, if the mind had any feelings; which it hasn't. It is merely a thermometer: it registers the heat and the cold, and cares not a farthing about either.

Y. M. Then we must not claim that if a man *knows* which of two things is right he is absolutely *bound* to do that thing?

O. M. His temperament and training will decide what he shall do, and he will do it; he cannot help himself, he has no authority over the matter. Wasn't it right for David to go out and slay Goliath?

Y. M. Yes.

O. M. Then it would have been equally *right* for any one else to do it?

Y. M. Certainly.

O. M. Then it would have been *right* for a born coward to attempt it?

Y. M. It would—yes.

O. M. You know that no born coward ever would have attempted it, don't you?

Y. M. Yes.

O. M. You know that a born coward's make and temperament would be an absolute and insurmountable bar to his ever essaying such a thing, don't you?

Y. M. Yes, I know it.

O. M. He clearly perceives that it would be *right* to try it?

Y. M. Yes.

O. M. His mind has Free Choice in determining that it would be *right* to try it?

Y. M. Yes.

O. M. Then if by reason of his inborn cowardice he simply can *not* essay it, what becomes of his Free Will? Where is his Free Will? Why claim that he has Free Will when the plain facts show that he hasn't? Why contend that because he and David *see* the right alike, both must *act* alike? Why impose the same laws upon goat and lion?

Y. M. There is really no such thing as Free Will?

O. M. It is what I think. There is *Will*. But it has nothing to do with *intellectual perceptions of right and wrong*, and is not under their command. David's temperament and training had Will, and it was a compulsory force; David had to obey its decrees, he had no choice. The coward's temperament and training possess Will, and *it* is compulsory; it commands him to avoid danger, and he obeys, he has no choice. But neither the

Davids nor the cowards possess Free Will—will that may do the right or do the wrong, as their mental verdict shall decide.

## Not Two Values, But Only One

Y. M. There is one thing which bothers me: I can't tell where you draw the line between material covetousness and spiritual covetousness.

O. M. I don't draw any.

Y. M. How do you mean?

O. M. There is no such thing as material covetousness. All covetousness is spiritual.

Y. M. *All* longings, desires, ambitions *spiritual*, never material?

O. M. Yes. The Master in you requires that in *all* cases you shall content his *spirit*—that alone. He never requires anything else, he never interests himself in any other matter.

Y. M. Ah, come! When he covets somebody's money—isn't that rather distinctly material and gross?

O. M. No. The money is merely a symbol—it represents in visible and concrete form a *spiritual desire.* Any so-called material thing that you want is merely a symbol: you want it not for *itself*, but because it will content your spirit for the moment.

Y. M. Please particularize.

O. M. Very well. Maybe the thing longed for is a new hat. You get it and your vanity is pleased, your spirit contented. Suppose your friends deride the hat, make fun of it: at once it loses its value; you are ashamed of it, you put it out of your sight, you never want to see it again.

Y. M. I think I see. Go on.

O. M. It is the same hat, isn't it? It is in no way altered. But it wasn't the *hat* you wanted, but only what it stood for—a something to please and content your *spirit.* When it failed of that, the whole of its value was gone. There are no *material* values; there are only spiritual ones. You will hunt in vain for a material value that is *actual, real*—there is no such thing. The only value it possesses, for even a moment, is the spiritual value back of it: remove that and it is at once worthless—like the hat.

Y. M. Can you extend that to money?

O. M. Yes. It is merely a symbol, it has no *material* value; you think you desire it for its own sake, but it is not so. You desire it for the spiritual content it will bring; if it fail of that, you discover that its value is gone. There is that pathetic tale of the man who labored like a slave, unresting, unsatisfied, until he had accumulated a fortune, and was happy over it, jubilant about it; then in a single week a pestilence swept away all whom he held dear and left him desolate. His money's value was gone. He realized that his joy in it came not from the money itself, but from the spiritual contentment he got out of his family's enjoyment of the pleasures and delights it lavished upon them. Money has no *material* value; if you remove its spiritual value nothing is left but dross. It is so with all things, little or big, majestic or trivial—there are no exceptions. Crowns, scepters, pennies, paste jewels, village notoriety, world-wide fame—they are all the same, they have no *material* value: while they content the *spirit* they are precious, when this fails they are worthless.

## *A Difficult Question*

Y. M. You keep me confused and perplexed all the time by your elusive terminology. Sometimes you divide a man up into two or three separate personalities, each with authorities, jurisdictions, and responsibilities of its own, and when he is in that condition I can't grasp him. Now when *I* speak of a man, he is *the whole thing in one*, and easy to hold and contemplate.

O. M. That is pleasant and convenient, if true. When you speak of "my body" who is the "my"?

Y. M. It is the "me."

O. M. The body is a property, then, and the Me owns it. Who is the Me?

Y. M. The Me is *the whole thing*; it is a common property; an undivided ownership, vested in the whole entity.

O. M. If the Me admires a rainbow, is it the whole Me that admires it, including the hair, hands, heels, and all?

Y. M. Certainly not. It is my *mind* that admires it.

O. M. So *you* divide the Me yourself. Everybody does; everybody must. What, then, definitely, is the Me?

Y. M. I think it must consist of just those two parts—the body and the mind.

O. M. You think so? If you say "I believe the world is round," who is the "I" that is speaking?

Y. M. The mind.

O. M. If you say "I grieve for the loss of my father," who is the "I"?

Y. M. The mind.

O. M. Is the mind exercising an intellectual function when it examines and accepts the evidence that the world is round?

Y. M. Yes.

O. M. Is it exercising an intellectual function when it grieves for the loss of your father?

Y. M. No. That is not cerebration, brain-work, it is a matter of *feeling*.

O. M. Then its source is not in your mind, but in your *moral* territory?

Y. M. I have to grant it.

O. M. Is your mind a part of your *physical* equipment?

Y. M. No. It is independent of it; it is spiritual.

O. M. Being spiritual, it cannot be affected by physical influences?

Y. M. No.

O. M. Does the mind remain sober when the body is drunk?

Y. M. Well—no.

O. M. There *is* a physical effect present, then?

Y. M. It looks like it.

O. M. A cracked skull has resulted in a crazy mind. Why should that happen if the mind is spiritual, and *independent* of physical influences?

Y. M. Well—I don't know.

O. M. When you have a pain in your foot, how do you know it?

Y. M. I feel it.

O. M. But you do not feel it until a nerve reports the hurt to the brain. Yet the brain is the seat of the mind, is it not?

Y. M. I think so.

O. M. But isn't spiritual enough to learn what is happening in the outskirts without the help of the *physical* messenger? You perceive that the question of who or what the Me is, is not a simple one at all. You say "I admire the rainbow," and "I believe the world is round," and in these cases we find that the Me is not all speaking, but only the *mental* part. You say "I grieve," and again the Me is not all speaking, but only the *moral* part. You say the mind is wholly spiritual; then you say "I have a pain" and find that this time the Me is mental *and* spiritual combined. We all use the "I" in this indeterminate fashion, there is no help for it. We imagine a Master and King over what you call The Whole Thing, and we speak of him as "I," but when we try to define him we find we cannot do it. The intellect and the feelings can act quite *independently* of each other; we recognize that, and we look around for a Ruler who is master over both, and can serve as a *definite and indisputable* "I," and enable us to know what we mean and who or what we are talking about when we use that pronoun, but we have to give it up and confess that we cannot find him. To me, Man is a machine, made up of many mechanisms, the moral and mental ones acting automatically in accordance with the impulses of an interior Master who is built out of born-temperament and an accumulation of multitudinous outside influences and trainings; a machine whose *one* function is to secure the spiritual contentment of the Master, be his desires good or be they evil; a machine whose Will is absolute and must be obeyed, and always *is* obeyed.

Y. M. Maybe the Me is the Soul?

O. M. Maybe it is. What is the Soul?

Y. M. I don't know.

O. M. Neither does any one else.

### The Master Passion

Y. M. What is the Master?—or, in common speech, the Conscience? Explain it.

O. M. It is that mysterious autocrat, lodged in a man, which compels the man to content its desires. It may be called the Master Passion—the hunger for Self-Approval.

Y. M. Where is its seat?

O. M. In man's moral constitution.

Y. M. Are its commands for the man's good?

O. M. It is indifferent to the man's good; it never concerns itself about anything but the satisfying of own desires. It can be *trained* to prefer things which will be for the man's good, but it will prefer them only because they will content *it* better than other things would.

Y. M. Then even when it is trained to high ideals it is still looking out for its own contentment, and not for the man's good?

O. M. True. Trained or untrained, it cares nothing for the man's good, and never concerns itself about it.

Y. M. It seems to be an *immoral* force seated in the man's moral constitution?

O. M. It is a *colorless* force seated in the man's moral constitution. Let us call it an instinct—a blind, unreasoning instinct, which cannot and does not distinguish between good morals and bad ones, and cares nothing for results to the man provided its own contentment be secured; and it will *always* secure that.

Y. M. It seeks money, and it probably considers that that is an advantage for the man?

O. M. It is not always seeking money, it is not always seeking power, nor office, nor any other *material* advantage. In *all* cases it seeks a *spiritual* contentment, let the *means* be what they may. Its desires are determined by the man's temperament—and it is lord over that. Temperament, Conscience, Susceptibility, Spiritual Appetite, are, in fact, the same thing. Have you ever heard of a person who cared nothing for money?

Y. M. Yes. A scholar who would not leave his garret and his books to take a place in a business house at a large salary.

O. M. He had to satisfy his master—that is to say, his temperament, his Spiritual Appetite—and it preferred the books to money. Are there other cases?

Y. M. Yes, the hermit.

O. M. It is a good instance. The hermit endures solitude, hunger, cold, and manifold perils, to content his autocrat, who prefers these things, and prayer and contemplation, to money or to any show or luxury that money can buy. Are there others?

Y. M. Yes. The artist, the poet, the scientist.

O. M. Their autocrat prefers the deep pleasures of these occupations, either well paid or ill paid, to any others in the market, at any price. You *realize* that the Master Passion—the contentment of the spirit—concerns itself with many things besides socalled material advantage, material prosperity, cash, and all that?

Y. M. I think I must concede it.

O. M. I believe you must. There are perhaps as many Temperaments that would refuse the burdens and vexations and distinctions of public office as there are that hunger after them. The one set of Temperaments seek the contentment of the spirit, and that alone; and this is exactly the case with the other set. Neither set seeks anything *but* the contentment of the spirit. If the one is sordid, both are sordid; and equally so, since the end in view is precisely the same in both cases. And in both cases Temperament decides the preference—and Temperament is *born*, not made.


## CONCLUSION


O. M. You have been taking a holiday?

Y. M. Yes; a mountain tramp covering a week. Are you ready to talk?

O. M. Quite ready. What shall we begin with?

Y. M. Well, lying abed resting up, two days and nights, I have thought over all these talks, and passed them carefully in review. With this result: that . . . that . . . are you intending to publish your notions about Man some day?

O. M. Now and then, in these past twenty years, the Master inside of me has half-intended to order me to set them to paper and publish them. Do I have to tell you why the order has remained unissued, or can you explain so simple a thing without my help?

Y. M. By your doctrine, it is simplicity itself: outside influences moved your interior Master to give the order; stronger outside influences deterred him. Without the outside influences, neither of these impulses could ever have been born, since a person's brain is incapable of originating an idea within itself.

O. M. Correct. Go on.

Y. M. The matter of publishing or withholding is still in your Master's hands. If some day an outside influence shall determine him to publish, he will give the order, and it will be obeyed.

O. M. That is correct. Well?

Y. M. Upon reflection I have arrived at the conviction that the publication of your doctrines would be harmful. Do you pardon me?

O. M. Pardon *you*? You have done nothing. You are an instrument—a speaking-trumpet. Speaking-trumpets are not responsible for what is said through them. Outside influences—in the form of lifelong teachings, trainings, notions, prejudices, and other second-hand importations—have persuaded the Master within you that the publication of these doctrines would be harmful. Very well, this is quite natural, and was to be expected; in fact, was inevitable. Go on; for the sake of ease and convenience, stick to habit: speak in the first person, and tell me what your Master thinks about it.

Y. M. Well, to begin: it is a desolating doctrine; it is not inspiring, enthusing, uplifting. It takes the glory out of man, it takes the pride out of him, it takes the heroism out of him, it denies him all personal credit, all applause; it not only degrades him to a machine, but allows him no control over the machine; makes a mere coffee-mill of him, and neither permits him to supply the coffee nor turn the crank, his sole and piteously humble function being to grind coarse or fine, according to his make, outside impulses doing all the rest.

O. M. It is correctly stated. Tell me—what do men admire most in each other?

Y. M. Intellect, courage, majesty of build, beauty of countenance, charity, benevolence, magnanimity, kindliness, heroism, and—and—

O. M. I would not go any further. These are *elementals*. Virtue, fortitude, holiness, truthfulness, loyalty, high ideals—these, and all the related qualities that are named in the dictionary, are *made of the elementals*, by blendings, combinations, and shadings of the elementals, just as one makes green by blending blue and yellow, and makes several shades and tints of red by modifying the elemental red. There are seven elemental colors; they are all in the rainbow; out of them we manufacture and name fifty shades of them. You have named the elementals of the human rainbow, and also one *blend*—heroism, which is made out of courage and magnanimity. Very well, then; which of these elements does the possessor of it manufacture for himself? Is it intellect?

Y. M. No.

O. M. Why?

Y. M. He is born with it.

O. M. Is it courage?

Y. M. No. He is born with it.

O. M. Is it majesty of build, beauty of countenance?

Y. M. No. They are birthrights.

O. M. Take those others—the elemental moral qualities—charity, benevolence, magnanimity, kindliness; fruitful seeds, out of which spring, through cultivation by outside influences, all the manifold blends and combinations of virtues named in the dictionaries: does man manufacture any one of those seeds, or are they all born in him?

Y. M. Born in him.

O. M. Who manufactures them, then?

Y. M. God.

O. M. Where does the credit of it belong?

Y. M. To God.

O. M. And the glory of which you spoke, and the applause?

Y. M. To God.

O. M. Then it is *you* who degrade man. You make him claim glory, praise, flattery, for every valuable thing he possesses—*borrowed* finery, the whole of it; no rag of it earned by himself, not a detail of it produced by his own labor. *You* make man a humbug; have I done worse by him?

Y. M. You have made a machine of him.

O. M. Who devised that cunning and beautiful mechanism, a man's hand?

Y. M. God.

O. M. Who devised the law by which it automatically hammers out of a piano an elaborate piece of music, without error, while the man is thinking about something else, or talking to a friend?

Y. M. God.

O. M. Who devised the blood? Who devised the wonderful machinery which automatically drives its renewing and refreshing streams through the body, day and night, without assistance or advice from the man? Who devised the man's mind, whose machinery works automatically, interests itself in what it pleases, regardless of his will or desire, labors all night, when it likes, deaf to his appeals for mercy? God devised all these things. *I* have not made man a machine, God made him a machine. I am merely calling attention to the fact, nothing more. Is it wrong to call attention to the fact? Is it a crime?

Y. M. I think it is wrong to *expose* a fact when harm can come of it.

O. M. Go on.

Y. M. Look at the matter as it stands now. Man has been taught that he is the supreme marvel of the Creation; he believes it; in all the ages he has never doubted it, whether he was a naked savage, or clothed in purple and fine linen, and civilized. This has made his heart buoyant, his life cheery. His pride in himself, his sincere admiration of himself, his joy in what he supposed were his own and unassisted achievements, and his exultation over the praise and applause which they evoked—these have exalted him, enthused him, ambitioned him to higher and higher flights; in a word, made his life worth living. But by your scheme, all this is abolished; he is degraded to a machine, he is a nobody, his noble prides wither to mere vanities; let him strive as he may, he can never be any better than his humblest and stupidest neighbor; he would never be cheerful again, his life would not be worth the living.

O. M. You really think that?

Y. M. I certainly do.

O. M. Have you ever seen me uncheerful, unhappy?

Y. M. No.

O. M. Well, *I* believe these things. Why have they not made me unhappy?

Y. M. Oh, well—temperament, of course! You never let *that* escape from your scheme.

O. M. That is correct. If a man is born with an unhappy temperament, nothing can make him happy; if he is born with a happy temperament nothing can make him unhappy.

Y. M. What—not even a degrading and heart-chilling system of beliefs?

O. M. Beliefs? Mere beliefs? Mere convictions? They are powerless. They strive in vain against inborn temperament.

Y. M. I can't believe that, and I don't.

O. M. Now you are speaking hastily. It shows that you have not studiously examined the facts. Of all your intimates, which one is the happiest? Isn't it Burgess?

Y. M. Easily.

O. M. And which one is the unhappiest? Henry Adams?[17]

Y. M. Without a question!

O. M. I know them well. They are extremes, abnormals; their temperaments are as opposite as the poles. Their life-histories are about alike—but look at the results! Their ages are about the same—around about fifty. Burgess has always been buoyant, hopeful, happy; Adams has always been cheerless, hopeless, despondent. As young fellows both tried country journalism—and failed. Burgess didn't seem to mind it; Adams couldn't smile, he could only mourn and groan over what had happened and torture himself with vain regrets for not having done so and so instead of so and so—*then* he would have succeeded. They tried the law—and failed. Burgess remained happy—because he couldn't help it. Adams was wretched—because he couldn't help it. From that day to this, those two men have gone on trying things and failing: Burgess has come out happy and cheerful every time; Adams the reverse. And we do absolutely know that these men's inborn temperaments have remained unchanged through all the vicissitudes of their material affairs. Let us see how it is with their immaterials. Both have been zealous Democrats; both have been zealous Republicans; both have been zealous Mugwumps.[18] Burgess has always found happiness and Adams unhappiness in these several political beliefs and in their migrations out of them. Both of these men have been Presbyterians, Universalists, Methodists, Catholics—then Presbyterians again, then Methodists again. Burgess has always found rest in these excursions, and Adams unrest. They are trying Christian Science, now, with the customary result, the inevitable result. No political or religious belief can make Burgess unhappy or the other man happy. I assure you it is purely a matter of temperament. Beliefs are *acquirements*, temperaments are *born*; beliefs are subject to change, nothing whatever can change temperament.

Y. M. You have instanced extreme temperaments.

O. M. Yes. The half-dozen others are modifications of the extremes. But the law is the same. Where the temperament is two-thirds happy, or two-thirds unhappy, no political or religious beliefs can change the proportions. The vast majority of temperaments are pretty equally balanced; the intensities are absent, and this enables a nation to learn to accommodate itself to its political and religious circumstances and like them, be satisfied with them, at last prefer them. Nations do not *think*, they only *feel*. They get their feelings at second hand through their temperaments, not their brains. A nation can be brought—by force of circumstances, not argument—to reconcile itself to *any kind of government or religion that can be devised*; in time it will fit itself to the required conditions; later, it will prefer them and will fiercely fight for them. As instances, you have all history: the Greeks, the Romans, the Persians, the Egyptians, the Russians, the Germans, the French, the English, the Spaniards, the Americans, the South Americans, the Japanese, the Chinese, the Hindoos, the Turks—a thousand wild and tame religions, every kind of government that can be thought of, from tiger to house-cat, each nation *knowing* it has the only true religion and the only sane system of government, each despising all the others, each an ass and not suspecting it, each proud of its fancied supremacy, each perfectly sure it is the pet of God, each with undoubting confidence summoning Him to take command in time of war, each surprised when He goes over to the enemy, but by habit able to excuse it and resume compliments—in a word, the whole human race content, always content, persistently content, indestructibly content, happy, thankful, proud, *no matter what its religion is, nor whether its master be tiger or house-cat.* Am I stating facts? You know I am. Is the human race cheerful? You know it is. Considering what it can stand, and be happy, you do me too much honor when you think that I can place before it a system of plain cold facts that can take the cheerfulness out of it. Nothing can do that. Everything has been tried. Without success. I beg you not to be troubled.

## NOTES

1. The Bessemer process was named after Sir Henry Bessemer (1813–1898), a British inventor and engineer, but it was developed and refined by several others. It is a process of removing impurities from pig-iron by the use of oxygen and heat. Its development led to the mass production of steel.

2. *Gobelin loom* refers to the Gobelins, a renowned French family of dyers and clothmakers beginning with Jehan Gobelin (d. 1476) and continuing through several generations of his descendants.

3. The Victoria Cross, the highest decoration for military valor in the British Empire, was established by Queen Victoria in 1856.

4. Alexander Hamilton (1755/57–1804), the first secretary of the treasury (1789–95), fought a duel with Aaron Burr (then vice president), on July 11, 1804, and died the next day, leaving his wife and seven children heavily in debt.

5. Twain refers to the work of American historian Francis Parkman (1823–1893), specifically *The Jesuits in North America in the Seventeenth Century* (1867).

6. The University Settlement was the first settlement house (a place where educated people could fraternize with the working classes for mutual benefit) in the United States. It opened in 1886 in the Lower East Side of New York City.

7. Millerites were the followers of William Miller (1782–1849), an American religious leader who maintained that the second coming of Christ, and hence the end of the world, would occur in 1843. He attracted up to one hundred thousand devotees.

8. Twain refers to Ignatius of Loyola (1491–1556), a Spanish knight who was hit by a cannonball in 1521 and broke his leg—an accident that ultimately led to a spiritual awakening and impelled him to found the Jesuits in 1539.

9. Alexander Pope, *An Essay on Man* (1733–34), 4.248.

10. Twain refers to a popular song, "In the Sweet Bye and Bye" (1902), words by Vincent P. Bryan, music by Harry von Tolzer. There is also a religious hymn of this title.

11. H. G. Wells, *The Invisible Man* (1897).

12. Twain refers to the conventional (but possibly apocryphal) story of how Scottish inventor James Watt (1736–1819) came upon the idea of the power of steam, leading to his invention of the steam engine in 1765.

13. The Marquess of Worcester had done all of this more than a century earlier. [MT] [Twain refers to Edward Somerset, second Marquess of Worcester (1601–1667), who claimed to have invented a rudimentary steam engine.]

14. Twain contrasts the quality of the clocks made in Strasbourg (in Alsace-Lorrain) and those made in Waterbury, Connecticut, chiefly in the early nineteenth century.

15. Twain refers to the experiments of British naturalist Sir John Lubbock, first baron Avebury (1834–1913), as found in such works as *The Origin and Metamorphosis of Insects* (1873) and *Ants, Bees and Wasps* (1882).

16. Francisco Pizarro (1475?–1541), Spanish explorer who ruthlessly subdued the native tribes of Peru in claiming the country for Spain.

17. Both Burgess and Henry Adams are fictitious. Burgess is a character in Twain's story "The Man That Corrupted Hadleyburg" (1899). As for Henry Adams, some scholars have believed that Twain is referring to the celebrated American historian and autobiographer of that name (1838–1918), who apparently did indeed have a somewhat lugubrious outlook on life; but a character of that name appears in "The £1,000,000 Bank-Note" (1893).

18. The term Mugwump was originally coined to designate those Republicans who refused to support their party's presidential candidate, James G. Blaine, in the election of 1884. It later came to denote anyone of a rebellious or contrarian spirit.

# REFLECTIONS ON THE SABBATH
## (1866)

The day of rest comes but once a week, and sorry I am that it does not come oftener. Man is so constituted that he can stand more rest than this. I often think regretfully that it would have been so easy to have two Sundays in a week, and yet it was not so ordained. The omnipotent Creator could have made the world in three days just as easily as he made it in six, and this would have doubled the Sundays. Still it is not our place to criticise the wisdom of the Creator. When we feel a depraved inclination to question the judgment of Providence in stacking up double eagles in the coffers of Michael Reese[1] and leaving better men to dig for a livelihood, we ought to stop and consider that we are not expected to help order things, and so drop the subject. If all-powerful Providence grew weary after six days' labor, such worms as we are might reasonably expect to break down in three, and so require two Sundays—but as I said before, it ill becomes us to hunt up flaws in matters which are so far out of our jurisdiction. I hold that no man can meddle with the exclusive affairs of Providence and offer suggestions for their improvement, without making himself in a manner conspicuous. Let us take things as we find them—though, I am free to confess, it goes against the grain to do it, sometimes.

What put me into this religious train of mind, was attending church at Dr. Wadsworth's this morning.[2] I had not been to church before for many months, because I never could get a pew, and therefore had to sit in the gallery, among the sinners. I stopped that because my proper place was down among the elect, inasmuch as I was brought up a Presbyterian, and consider myself a brevet member of Dr. Wadsworth's church. I always was a brevet. I was sprinkled in infancy, and look upon that as conferring the rank of Brevet Presbyterian. It affords none of the emoluments of the Regular Church—simply confers honorable rank upon the recipient and the right to be punished as a Presbyterian hereafter, that is, the substantial Presbyterian punishment of fire and brimstone instead of this heterodox hell of remorse of conscience of these blamed wildcat religions. The heaven and hell of the wildcat religions are vague and ill defined but there is nothing mixed about the Presbyterian heaven and hell. The Presbyterian hell is all misery; the heaven all happiness—nothing to do. But when a man dies on a wildcat basis, he will never rightly know hereafter which department he is in—but he will think he is in hell anyhow, no matter which place he goes to; because in the good place they pro-gress, pro-gress, pro-gress—study, study, study, all the time—and if this isn't hell I dont know what is; and in the bad place he will be worried by remorse of conscience. Their bad place is preferable, though, because eternity is long, and before a man got half through it he would forget what it was he had been so sorry about. Naturally he would then become cheerful again; but the party who went to heaven would go on progressing and progressing, and studying and studying until he would finally get discouraged and wish he were in hell, where he wouldn't require such a splendid education.

Dr. Wadsworth never fails to preach an able sermon; but every now and then, with an admirable assumption of not being aware of it, he will get off a firstrate joke and then frown severely at any one who is surprised into smiling at it. This is not fair. It is like throwing a bone to a dog and then arresting him with a look just as he is going to seize it. Several people there on Sunday suddenly laughed and as suddenly stopped again, when he gravely gave the Sunday school books a blast and spoke of "the good little boys in them who always went to Heaven, and the bad little boys who infallibly got drowned on Sunday," and then swept a savage frown around the house and blighted every smile in the congregation.

## NOTES

1. Michael Reese was a wealthy San Francisco businessman involved in a number of unsavory financial transactions as well as a breach of promise suit in

1866–67. See Charles H. Cutter, "Michael Reese: Parsimonious Patron of the University of California," *California Historical Society Quarterly* 42 (1963): 127–44.

2. Charles Wadsworth (1814–1882) was a Presbyterian minister whose departure from Philadelphia to the Calvary Church in San Francisco in 1861 was a blow to Emily Dickinson, who was apparently in love with him.

# ABOUT SMELLS
## (1870)

*I*n a recent issue of the "Independent," the Rev. T. De Witt Talmage,[1] of Brooklyn, has the following utterance on the subject of "Smells":

> I have a good Christian friend who, if he sat in the front pew in church, and a working man should enter the door at the other end, would smell him instantly. My friend is not to blame for the sensitiveness of his nose, any more than you would flog a pointer being keener on the scent than a stupid watch-dog. The fact is, if you had all the churches free, by reason of the mixing up of the common people with the uncommon, you would keep onehalf of Christendom sick at their stomach. If you are going to kill the church thus with bad smells, I will have nothing to do with this work of evangelization.

We have reason to believe that there will be laboring men in heaven; and also a number of negroes, and Esquimaux, and Terra del Fuegans, and Arabs, and a few Indians, and possibly even some Spaniards and Portuguese. All things are possible with God. We shall have all these sorts of people in heaven; but, alas! in getting them we shall lose the society of Dr. Talmage. Which is to say, we shall lose the company of one who could give more real "tone" to celestial society than any other contribution Brooklyn could furnish. And what would eternal happiness be without the Doctor? Blissful, unquestionably—we know that well enough—but would it be *distingué*, would it be *recherché* without him, St. Matthew without stockings or sandals; St. Jerome bareheaded, and with a coarse brown blanket robe dragging the ground; St. Sebastian with scarcely any raiment at all—these we should see, and should enjoy seeing them; but would we not miss a spike-tailed coat and kids, and turn away regretfully, and say to parties from the Orient: "These are well enough, but you ought to see Talmage of Brooklyn." I fear me that in the better world we shall not even have Dr. Talmage's "good Christian friend." For if he were sitting under the glory of the Throne, and the keeper of the keys admitted a Benjamin Franklin or other laboring man, that "friend," with his fine natural powers infinitely augmented by emancipation from hampering flesh, would detect him with a single sniff, and immediately take his hat and ask to be excused.

To all outward seeming, the Rev. T. De Witt Talmage is of the same material as that used in the construction of his early predecessors in the ministry; and yet one feels that there must be a difference somewhere between him and the Savior's first disciples. It may be because here, in the nineteenth century, Dr. T. has had advantages which Paul and Peter and the others could not and did not have. There was a lack of polish about them, and a looseness of etiquette, and a want of exclusiveness, which one cannot help noticing. They healed the very beggars, and held entercourse with people of a villanous odor every day. If the subject of these remarks had been chosen among the original Twelve Apostles, he would not have associated with the rest, because he could not have stood the fishy smell of some of his comrades who came from around the Sea of Galilee. He would have resigned his commission with some such remark as he makes in the extract quoted above: "Master, if thou art going to kill the church thus with bad smells, I will have nothing to do with this work of evangelization." He is a disciple, and makes that remark to the Master; the only difference is, that he makes it in the nineteenth instead of the first century.

Is there a choir in Mr. T.'s church? And does it ever occur that they have no better manners than to sing that hymn which is so suggestive of laborers and mechanics:

> "Son of the Carpenter! Receive
> This humble work of mine?"

Now, can it be possible that in a handful of centuries the Christian character has fallen away from an imposing heroism that scorned even the stake, the cross, and the axe, to a poor little effeminacy that withers and wilts under an unsavory smell? We are not prepared to believe so, the reverend Doctor and his friend to the contrary notwithstanding.

## NOTE

1. Thomas De Witt Talmage (1832–1902) was a Presbyterian minister and pastor at the Central Presbyterian Church in Brooklyn (1869–95). He was noted for his eloquence. The *Independent* was a Presbyterian paper.

# THE INDIGNITY PUT UPON THE REMAINS OF GEORGE HOLLAND BY THE REV. MR. SABINE

## (1871)

*W*hat a ludicrous satire it was upon Christian charity!—even upon the vague, theoretical idea of it which doubtless this small saint mouths from his own pulpit every Sunday. Contemplate this freak of Nature, and think what a Cardiff giant of self-righteousness is crowded into his pigmy skin. If we probe, and dissect, and lay open this diseased, this cancerous piety of his, we are forced to the conviction that it is the production of an impression on his part that his guild do about all the good that is done in the earth, and hence are better than common clay—hence are competent to say to such as George Holland,[1] "You are unworthy; you are a play-actor, and consequently a sinner; I cannot take the responsibility of recommending you to the mercy of Heaven." It must have had its origin in that impression, else he would have thought, "We are all instruments for the carrying out of God's purposes; it is not for me to pass judgment upon your appointed share of the work, or to praise or to revile it; I have divine authority for it that we are *all* sinners, and therefore it is not for me to discriminate and say we will supplicate for this sinner, for he was a merchant prince or a banker, but we will beseech no forgiveness for this other one, for he was a play-actor." It surely requires the farthest possible reach of self-righteousness to enable a man to lift his scornful nose in the air and turn his back upon so poor and pitiable a thing as a dead stranger come to beg the last kindness that humanity can do in its behalf. This creature has violated the letter of the gospel and judged George Holland—not George Holland either, but his profession through him. Then it is in a measure fair that we judge this creature's guild through him. In effect he has said, "We are the salt of the earth; we do all the good work that is done; to learn how to be good and do good, men must come to us; actors and such are obstacles to moral progress."[2] Pray look at the thing reasonably for a moment, laying aside all biasses of education and custom. If a common public impression is fair evidence of a thing, then the minister's legitimate, recognized, and acceptable business is to *tell* people calmly, coldly, and in stiff, written sentences, from the pulpit, to go and do right, be just, be merciful, be charitable. And his congregation forget it all between church and home. But for fifty years it was George Holland's business, on the stage, to *make* his audience go and do right, and be just, merciful, and charitable—because by his living, breathing, feeling pictures, he showed them what it *was* to do these things, and *how* to do them, and how instant and ample was the reward! Is it not a singular teacher of men, this reverend gentleman who is so poorly informed himself as to put the whole stage under ban, and say, "I do not think it teaches moral lessons"?

Where was ever a sermon preached that could make filial ingratitude so hateful to men as the sinful play of "King Lear"? Or where was there ever a sermon that could so convince men of the wrong and the cruelty of harboring a pampered and unanalyzed jealousy as the sinful play of "Othello"? And where are there ten preachers who can stand in the pulpit teaching heroism, unselfish devotion, and lofty patriotism, and hold their own against any one of five hundred William Tells that can be raised up upon five hundred stages in the land at a day's notice? It is almost fair and just to aver (although it is profanity) that nine-tenths of all the kindness and forbearance and Christian charity and generosity in the hearts of the American people to-day, got there by being filtered down from their fountain-head, the gospel of Christ, *through dramas and tragedies and comedies on the stage, and through the despised novel and the Christmas story, and through the thousand and one lessons, suggestions, and narratives of qenerous deeds that stir the pulses, and exalt and augment the nobility of the nation day by day from the teeming columns of ten thousand newspapers,* and not from the drowsy pulpit!

All that is great and good in our particular civilization came straight from the hand of Jesus Christ, and many creatures, and of divers sorts, were doubtless appointed to disseminate it; and let us believe that *this seed and the result* are the main thing, and not the cut of the sower's garment; and that whosoever, in his way and according to his opportunity, sows the one and produces the other, has done high service and worthy. And further, let us try with all our strength to believe that whenever old simple-hearted George Holland sowed this seed, and reared his crop of broader charities and better impulses in men's hearts, it was just as acceptable before the Throne as if the seed had been scattered in vapid platitudes from the pulpit of the ineffable Sabine himself.

Am I saying that the pulpit does not do its share toward disseminating the marrow, the *meat* of the gospel of Christ? (For we are not talking of ceremonies and wire-drawn creeds now, but the living heart and soul of what is pretty often only a spectre.)

No, I am not saying that. The pulpit reaches assemblages of people twice a week—nearly two hours, altogether—and does what it can in that time. The theatre teaches large audiences seven times a week—28 or 30 hours altogether, and the novels and newspapers plead, and argue, and illustrate, stir, move, thrill, thunder, urge, persuade, and supplicate, at the feet of millions and millions of people every single day, and all day long, and far into the night; and so these vast agencies till *nine-tenths* of the vineyard, and the pulpit tills the other tenth. Yet now and then some complacent blind idiot says, "You unanointed are coarse clay and useless, you are not as we, the regenerators of the world; go, bury yourselves elsewhere, for we cannot take the responsibility of recommending idlers and sinners to the yearning mercy of Heaven." How does a soul like that stay in a carcass without getting mixed with the secretions and sweated out through the pores? Think of this insect condemning the whole theatrical service as a disseminator of bad morals because it has Black Crooks in it;[3] forgetting that if that were sufficient ground, people would condemn the pulpit because it had Cooks, and Kallochs,[4] and Sabines in it.

No, I am not trying to rob the pulpit of any atom of its full share and credit in the work of disseminating the meat and marrow of the gospel of Christ; but I am trying to get a moment's hearing for worthy agencies in the same work, that with overwrought modesty seldom or never claim a recognition of their great services. I am aware that the pulpit does its excellent one-tenth (and credits itself with it now and then, though most of the time a press of business causes it to forget it); I am aware that in its honest and well-meaning way it bores the people with uninflammable truisms about doing good; bores them with correct compositions on charity; bores them, chloroforms them, stupefies them with argumentative mercy without a flaw in the grammar, or an emotion which the minister could put in in the right place if he turned his back and took his finger off the manuscript. And in doing these things the pulpit is doing its duty, and let us believe that it is likewise doing its best, and doing it in the most harmless and respectable way. And so I have said, and shall keep on saying, let us give the pulpit its full share of credit in elevating and ennobling the people; but when a pulpit takes to itself authority to pass judgment upon the work and the worth of just as legitimate an instrument of God as itself, who spent a long life preaching from the stage the self-same gospel without the alteration of a single sentiment or a single axiom of right, it is fair and just that somebody who believes that actors were made for a high and good purpose, and that they *accomplish the object of their creation* and accomplish it well, to protest. And having protested, it is also fair and just—being driven to it, as it were—to whisper to the Sabine pattern of clergyman, under the breath, a simple, instructive truth, and say, "Ministers are not the only servants of God upon earth, nor His most efficient ones either, by a very, very long distance!" Sensible ministers already know this, and it may do the other kind good to find it out.

But to cease teaching and go back to the beginning again, was it not pitiable, that spectacle? Honored and honorable old George Holland, whose theatrical ministry had for fifty years softened hard hearts, bred generosity in cold ones, kindled emotion in dead ones, uplifted base ones, broadened bigoted ones, and made many and many a stricken one glad and filled it brim full of gratitude, figuratively spit upon in his unoffending coffin by this crawling, slimy, sanctimonious, self-righteous reptile!

## NOTES

1. George Holland (1791–1870) was a British-born actor who emigrated to the United States in 1827 and worked in theaters across the country, mostly in "low" comedies and farces. Upon his death, the Reverend William Sabine (1838–1913), Episcopal pastor of the Church of the Atonement in New York City and later a bishop, created a furor by refusing to preside over his funeral service.

2. Reporter—What answer did you make, Mr. Sabine?

Mr. Sabine—I said that I had a distaste for officiating at such a funeral, and that I did not care to be mixed up in it. I said to the gentleman that I was willing to bury the deceased from his house, but that I objected to having the funeral solemnized at a church.

Reporter—Is it one of the laws of the Protestant Episcopal Church that a deceased theatrical performer shall not be buried from the church?

Mr. Sabine—It is not, but I have always warned the professing members of my congregation to keep away from theatres and not to have anything to do with them. I don't think that they teach moral lessons.—*New York Times.* [MT] [The quotation is from the article "Pharisaical Delicacy," *New York Times* (29 December 1870): 1.]

3. Twain refers to the 1866 musical *The Black Crook* (book by Charles M. Barras; music and lyrics by Thomas Baker and others), featuring a character named Hertzog, the Black Crook, who seeks to capture human souls.

4. Horace Cook (1820?–1871), Methodist pastor in New York City who lost his position when he was detected seducing a parishioner's daughter. Isaac Kalloch (1831–1887), Baptist minister in Boston who was tried for adultery in 1857. He later became minister of the Metropolitan Temple in San Francisco and mayor of San Francisco (1879–81).

# THE REVISED CATECHISM
## (1871)

*F*irst class in modern Moral Philosophy stand up and recite:

What is the chief end of man?

A. To get rich.

In what way?

A. Dishonestly if we can; honestly if we must.

Who is God, the one only and true?

A. Money is God. Gold and greenbacks and stock—father, son, and the ghost of the same—three persons in one: these are the true and only God, mighty and supreme; and William Tweed is his prophet.[1]

Name the twelve disciples.

A. St. Ass's Colt Hall, whereon the prophet rode into Jerusalem, St. Connolly, the beloved disciple; St. Matthew Carnochan, that sitteth at the receipt of customs; St. Peter Fisk the belligerent disciple; St. Paul Gould, that suffereth many stripes and glorieth in them; St. Iscariot Winans; St. Jacob Vanderbilt, the essteamed disciple; St. Garvey, the chair-itable; St. Ingersoll, of the holy carpets; St. N. Y. Printing Co., the meek and lowly, that letteth not its right hand know what its left hand taketh; St. Peter Hoffman, that denied his (Irish) master when the public cock had crowed six or seven times; St. Barnard, the wise judge, who imparteth injunctions in time of trouble, whereby the people are instructed to their salvation.[2]

How shall a man attain the chief end of life?

A. By furnishing imaginary carpets to the Court-House, apocryphal chairs to the armories, and invisible printing to the city.

Are there other ways?

A. Yea. By purchasing the quarantine apostle for a price; by lightering shipmen of all they possess; by proceeding through immigrants from over sea; by burying the moneyless at the public charge and transhipping the rest 10 miles at $40 a head. By testing iron work for buildings. By furnishing lead and iron gas-pipes to the Court-House and then conveying the impression in the bill that they were constructed of gold and silver and set with diamonds. By taking care of the public parks at $5 an inch. By loafing around gin mills on a salary under the illusion that you are imparting impetus to a shovel on the public works.

Are these sufficient? If not, what shall a man do else, to be saved?

A. Make out his bill for ten prices and deliver nine of them into the hands of the prophet and the holy family. Then shall he be saved.

Who were the models the young were taught to emulate in former days?

A. Washington and Franklin.

Whom do they and should they emulate now in this era of larger enlightenment?

A. Tweed, Hall, Connolly, Carnochan, Fisk, Gould, Barnard, and Winans.

What works were chiefly prized for the training of the young in former days?

Richard's Almanac, the Pilgrim's Progress,[3] and the Declaration of Independence.

What are the best prized Sunday-school books in this more enlightened age?

A. St. Hall's Garbled Reports, St. Fisk's Ingenious Robberies, St. Carnochan's Guide to Corruption, St. Gould on the Watering of Stock, St. Barnard's Injunctions, St. Tweed's Handbook of Morals, and the Court-House edition of the Holy Crusade of the Forty Thieves.

Do we progress?

A. You bet your life!


## NOTES

1. William ("Boss") Tweed (1823–1878), New York political leader who ran the corrupt political organization Tammany Hall from 1868 to 1871. He spent the rest of his life in and out of jail.

2. Twain refers to the following: Abraham Oakley Hall (1826–1898), mayor of New York (1868–72). Richard B. ("Slippery Dick") Connolly (1810–1880), New York City controller. Dr. John Murray Carnochan (1817–1887), quarantine health officer of New York suspected of corruption. James Fisk (1834–1872), financial speculator who with Jay Gould (1836–1892) was involved in several dubious attempts to make money on railroads, leading to Black Friday (September 24, 1869), a collapse of the stock market that led to a four-year depression. Orange S. Winans, Republican assemblyman from Chautauqua county accused of accepting bribes. Jacob Vanderbilt (1807–1893), brother of Cornelius Vanderbilt and owner of a steamship line who was indicted but never prosecuted for the explosion of one of his ferryboats in New York harbor on July 30, 1871. Andrew J. Garvey, New York City contractor. James H. Ingersoll, carpet and furniture supplier. New York Printing Co., a company owned by Boss Tweed that supplied paper products to the city. John T. Hoffman (1828–1888), governor of New York (1869–72) and mayor of New York City (1865–68). George G. Barnard (1824?–1879), judge of the New York State supreme court and a Tammany politician.

3. *Poor Richard's Almanac* (1733–58), a periodical established by Benjamin Franklin containing pithy axioms on life, especially regarding frugality; *The Pilgrim's Progress* (1678), religious allegory by John Bunyan.

# THE SECOND ADVENT
## (1881)

*B*lack Jack is a very small village lying far away back in the western wilds and solitudes of Arkansas. It is made up of a few log cabins; its lanes are deep with mud in wet weather; its fences and gates are rickety and decayed; its cornfields and gardens are weedy, slovenly, and poorly cared for; there are no newspapers, no railways, no factories, no library; ignorance, sloth and drowsiness prevail. There is a small log church, but no school. The hogs are many, and they wallow by the doors, they sun themselves in the public places.

It is a frontier village; the border of the Indian Territory[1] is not a day's walk away, and the loafing savage is a common sight in the town. There are some other sleepy villages thereabouts: Tumblinsonville, three or four miles off; Brunner, four or five; Sugarloaf, ten or twelve. In effect, the region is a solitude, and far removed from the busy world and the interests which animate it.

A gentle and comely young girl, Nancy Hopkins, lived in Black Jack, with her parents. The Hopkinses were old residents; in fact neither they nor their forerunners for two generations had ever known any other place than Black Jack. When Nancy was just budding into womanhood, she was courted by several of the young men of the village, but she finally gave the preference to Jackson Barnes the blacksmith, and was promised to him in marriage by her parents. This was soon known to everybody, and of course discussed freely, in village fashion. The young couple were chaffed, joked, and congratulated in the frank, rude, frontier way, and the discarded suitors were subjected to abundance of fat-witted raillery.

Then came a season of quiet, the subject being exhausted; a season wherein tongues were still, there being nothing whatever in that small world to talk about. But by and by a change came; suddenly all tongues were busy again. Busier, too, than they had ever been at any time before,

113

within any one's memory; for never before had they been furnisbed with anything like so prodigious a topic as now offered itself: Nancy Hopkins, the sweet young bride elect, was—

The news flew from lip to lip with almost telegraphic swiftness; wives told it to their husbands; husbands to bachelors; servants got hold of it and told it to the young misses; it was gossiped over in every corner; rude gross pioneers coarsely joked about it over their whisky in the village grocery, accompanying their witticisms with profane and obscene words and mighty explosions of horse laughter. The unsuspecting blacksmith was called into this grocery and the crushing news sprung upon him with a brutal frankness and directness. At first he was bowed with grief and misery; but very soon anger took the place of these feelings, and he went forth saying he would go and break the engagement. After he was gone, the grocery crowd organized itself into a public meeting to consider what ought to be done with the girl. After brief debate it was resolved—

1. That she must name her betrayer.
2. And immediately marry him.
3. Or be tarred and feathered and banished to the Indian Territory.

The proceedings were hardly ended when Jackson Barnes was seen returning; and, to the general astonishment, his face was seen to be calm, placid, content—even joyful. Everybody crowded around to hear what he might say in explanation of this strange result. There was a deep and waiting silence for some moments; then Barnes said solemnly, and with awe in his voice and manner:

"She has explained it. She has made everything clear. I am satisfied, and have taken her back to my love and protection. She has told me all, and with perfect frankness, concealing nothing. She is pure and undefiled. She will give birth to a son, but no man has had to do with her. God has honored her, God has overshadowed her, and to Him she will bear this child. A joy inexpressible is ours, for we are blessed beyond all mankind."

His face was radiant with a holy happiness while he spoke. Yet when he had finished a brutal jeer went up from the crowd, and everybody mocked at him, and he was assailed on all sides with insulting remarks and questions. One said—

"How does she know it was God?"

Barnes answered: "An angel told her."

"When did the angel tell her?"

"Several months ago."

"Before, or after the act?"

"Before."

"Told her it was going to happen?"

"Yes."

"Did she believe the angel at the time?"

"Yes."

"But didn't mention the matter to you at the time?"

"No."

"Why didn't she?"

"I do not know."

"Did she mention it to the old people?"

"No."

"Why didn't she?"

"I do not know."

"Had she any other evidence as to the facts than the angel?"

"No."

"What did the angel look like?"

"Like a man."

"Naked?"

"No—clothed."

"How?"

"In ancient times the angels came clothed in a robe, the dress of the people of the day. Naturally this one was clothed according to the fashion of our day. He wore a straw hat, a blue jeans roundabout and pants, and cowhide boots."

"How did she know he was an angel?"

"Because he said he was; and angels cannot lie."

"Did he speak English?"

"Of course; else she would not have understood him."

"Did he speak like an American, or with an accent?"

"He had no accent."

"Were there any witnesses?"

"No—she was alone."

"It might have been well to have some witnesses. Have you any evidence to convince you except her word?"

"Yes. While I talked with her, sleep came upon me for a moment, and I dreamed. In my dream I was assured by God that all she had said was true, and He also commanded me to stand by her and marry her."

"How do you know that the dream came from God and not from your dinner? How could you tell?"

"I knew because the voice of the dream distinctly said so."

"You believe, then, that Nancy Hopkins is still pure and undefiled?"

"I know it. She is still a virgin."

"Of course you may know that, and know it beyond doubt or question, if you have applied the right test. Have you done this?"

"I have not applied any test. I do not need to. I know perfectly that she is a virgin, by better evidence than a test."

"By what evidence? How can you know—how do you know—that she is still a virgin?"

"I know it because she told me so herself, with her own lips."

"Yes, and you dreamed it besides."

"I did."

"Absolutely overwhelming proof—isn't it?"

"It seems so to me."

"Isn't it possible that a girl might lie, in such circumstances, to save her good name?"

"To save her good name, yes; but to lie in this case would be to rob herself of the unspeakable honor of being made fruitful by Almighty God. It would be more than human heroism for Nancy Hopkins to lie, in this case, and deny the illustrious fatherhood of her child, and throw away the opportunity to make her name revered and renowned forever in the world. She did right to confess her relations with the Deity. Where is there a girl in Black Jack who would not be glad to enjoy a like experience, and proud to proclaim it?"

"You suspect none but God?"

"How should I?"

"You do not suspect the angel in the straw hat?"

"He merely brought the message, that is all."

"And delivered it and left immediately?"

"I suppose so. I do not know."

"Suppose he had staid away and sent it by mail—or per dream, which is cheaper and saves paper and postage—would the result to Nancy have been the same, do you think?"

"Of course; for the angel had nothing to do but convey the prophecy; his functions ceased there."

"Possibly they did. Still, it would be helpful to hear from the angel. What shall you do with this child when it comes?"

"I shall rear it carefully, and provide for it to the best of my means."

"And call it your own?"

"I would not dare to. It is the child of the most high God. It is holy."

"What shall you call it, if it be a girl?"

"It will not be a girl."

"Then if it be a boy?"

"It shall be called Jesus Christ."

"What—is there to be another Jesus Christ?"

"No, it is the same that was born of Mary, ages ago, not another. This is merely the Second Advent; I was so informed by the Most High in my dream."

"You are in error, manifestly. He is to come the second time not humbly, but in clouds and great glory."

"Yes, but that has all been changed. It was a question if the world would believe it was Jesus if he came in that way, so the former method was reinstituted. He is to be again born of an obscure Virgin, because the world cannot help but believe and be convinced by that circumstance, since it has been convinced by it before."

"To be frank with you, we do not believe a word of this flimsy nonsense you are talking. Nancy Hopkins has gone astray; she is a disgraced girl, and she knows it and you know it and we all know it. She must not venture to show her face among our virtuous daughters; we will not allow it. If you wish to marry her and make an honest woman of her, well and good; but take her away from here, at least till the wind of this great scandal has somewhat blown over."

So the Hopkinses and the blacksmith shut themselves up in their house, and were shunned and despised by the whole village.

But the day of their sorrow was to have an end, in time. They felt it, they knew it, in truth, for their dreams said it. So they waited, and were patient. Meantime the marvelous tale spread abroad; village after village heard of the new Virgin and the new Christ, and presently the matter traveled to the regions of newspapers and telegraphs; then instantly it swept the world as upon myriad wings, and was talked of in all lands.

So at last came certain wise men from the far east, to inquire concerning the matter, and to learn for themselves whether the tale was true or false. These were editors from New York and other great cities, and presidents of Yale and Princeton and Andover and other great colleges. They saw a star shining in the east—it was Venus—and this they resolved to follow. Several astronomers said that a star could not be followed—that a person might as well try to follow a spot on the sun's disk, or any other object that was so far away it could not be seen to move. Other astronomers said that if a star should come down low enough to be valuable as a guide, it would roof the whole earth in, and make total darkness and give forth no relieving light itself—and that then it would be just as useful, as a guide, as is the eternal roof of the Mammoth Cave to the explorer of its maze of halls and chambers. And they also said that a star could not descend thus low without disorganizing the universe and hurling all the worlds together in confusion.

But the wise men were not disturbed. They answered that what had happened once could happen again. And they were right. For this talk had hardly ended when Venus did actually leave her place in the sky and come down and hang over the very building in which the sages were assembled. She gave out a good light, too, and appeared to be no larger than a full moon.

The wise men were greatly rejoiced; and they gathered together their baggage, and their editorial passes, and clerical half-rate tickets, and took the night train westward praising God. In the morning they stopped at Pittsburg and laid over till Venus was visible again in the evening. And so they journeyed on, night after night. At Louisville they got news of the child's birth. That night they resumed their journey; and so continued, by rail and horse conveyance, following the star until it came and stood over the house in Black Jack where the young child lay. Then the star retired into the sky, and they saw it go back and resume its glimmering function in the remote east.

It was about dawn, now; and immediately the whole heavens were filled with flocks of descending angels, and these were joined by a choir of drovers who were ranching in the vicinity, and all broke forth into song—the angels using a tune of their own, and the others an Arkansas tune, but all employing the same words. The wise men assisted, as well as they could, until breakfast time; then the angels returned home, the drovers resumed business, and the wise men retired to the village tavern.

After breakfast, the wise men being assembled privately, the President of Princeton made a brief speech and offered this suggestion:

1. That they all go, in a body, to see the child and hear the evidence;
2. That they all question the witnesses and assist in sifting the testimony;
3. But that the verdict be voted and rendered, not by the full body, but by a jury selected out of by ballot.

Mr. Greeley, Mr. Bennett and Mr. Beach[2] saw no good reason for this. They said the whole body was as good a jury as a part of it could be.

The President of Princeton replied that the proposed method would simplify matters.

A vote was then taken and the measure carried, in spite of the editorial opposition.

The President of Andover then proposed that the jury consist of six persons, and that only members of some orthodox church be eligible.

Against this the editors loudly protested, and remarked that this would make a packed jury and rule out every editor, since none of their faction would be eligible. Mr. Greeley implored the President of Andover to relinquish his proposition; and reminded him that the church had always been accused of packing juries and using other underhand methods wherever its interests seemed to be concerned; and reminded him, further, as an instance, that church trials of accused clergymen nearly always resulted in a barefaced whitewashing of the accused. He begged that the present opportunity to improve the church's reputation would not be thrown away, but that a fair jury, selected without regard to religious opinion or complexion might be chosen.

The plea failed, however, and a jury composed solely of church members was chosen, the church faction being largely in the majority and voting as a unit. The editors were grieved over the advantage which had been taken of their numerical weakness, but they could not help themselves.

Then the wise men arose and went in a body to see the Hopkinses. There they listened to the evidence offered by Nancy and Barnes; and when the testimony was all in, it was examined and discussed. The religious faction maintained that it was clear, coherent, cogent, and without flaw, discrepancy, or doubtful feature; but the editorial faction stoutly maintained the directly opposite view, and implored the jury to consider well, and not allow their judgment to be influenced by prejudice and what might seem to be ecclesiastical interest.

The jury then retired; and after a brief absence brought in a verdict, as follows:

"We can doubt no whit. We find these to be the facts: An angel informed Nancy Hopkins of what was to happen; this is shown by her unqualified declaration. She is still a virgin; we know this is so, because we have her word for it. Tlie child is the actual child of Almighty God— a fact established by overwhelming testimony, to-wit, the testimony of the angel, of Nancy, and of God Himself, as delivered to Jackson Barnes in a dream. Our verdict, then, is that this child is truly the Christ the Son of God, that his birth is miraculous, and that his mother is still a virgin."

Then the jury and their faction fell upon their knees and worshiped the child, and laid at its feet costly presents: namely, a History of the Church's Dominion During the First Fourteen Centuries; a History of the Presbyterian Dominion in Scotland; a History of Catholic Dominion in England; a History of the Salem Witchcraft; a History of the Holy Inquisition; in addition, certain toys for the child to play with—these being tiny models of the Inquisition's instruments of torture; and a little Holy Bible with the decent passages printed in red ink.

But the other wise men, the editors, murmured and were not satisfied. Mr. Horace Greeley delivered their opinion. He said:

"Where an individual's life is at stake, hearsay evidence is not received in courts; how, then, shall we venture to receive hearsay evidence in this case, where the eternal life of whole nations is at stake? We have hearsay evidence that an angel appeared; none has seen that angel but one individual, and she an interested person. We have hearsay evidence that the angel delivered a certain message; whether it has come to us untampered with or not, we can never know, there being none to convey it to us but a party interested in having it take a certain form. We have the evidence of dreams and other hearsay evidence—and still, as before, from interested parties—that God is the father of this child, and that its mother remains a virgin: the first a statement which never has been and never will be possible of verification, and the last a statement which could only have been verified before the child's birth, but not having been done then can never hereafter be done. Silly dreams, and the unverifiable twaddle of a family of nobodies who are interested in covering up a young girl's accident and shielding her from disgrace—such is the 'evidence!' 'Evidence' like this could not affect even a dog's case, in any court in Christendom. It is rubbish, it is foolishness. No court would listen to it; it would be an insult to judge and jury to offer it."

Then a young man of the other party, named Talmage,[3] rose in a fury of generous enthusiasm, and denounced the last speaker as a reprobate and infidel, and said he had earned and would receive his right reward in the fulness of time in that everlasting hell created and appointed for his kind by this holy child, the God of the heavens and the earth and all that in them is. Then he sprang high in the air three times, cracking his heels together and praising God. And when he had finally alighted and become in a measure stationary, he shouted in a loud voice saying:

"Here is divine evidence, evidence from the lips of very God Himself, and it is scoffed at! here is evidence from an angel of God, coming fresh from the fields of heaven, from the shadow of the Throne, with the odors of Eternal Land upon his raiment, and it is derided! here is evidence from God's own chosen handmaid, holy and pure, whom He has fructified without sin, and it is mocked at! here is evidence of one who has spoken face to face with the Most High in a dream, and even his evidence is called lies and foolishness! and on top of all, here is *cumulative* evidence: for the fact that all these things have happened before, in exactly the same way, establishes the genuineness of this second happening beyond shadow or possibility of doubt to all minds not senile, idiotic or given hopelessly over to the possession of hell and the devil! If men cannot believe *these* evidences, taken together, and piled, Pelion on Ossa,[4] mountains high, what can they believe!"

Then the speaker flung himself down, with many contortions, and wallowed in the dirt before the child, singing praises and glorifying God.

The Holy Family remained at Black Jack, and in time the world ceased to talk about them, and they were forgotten.

But at the end of thirty years they came again into notice; for news went abroad that Jesus had begun to teach in the churches, and to do miracles. He appointed twelve disciples, and they went about proclaiming Christ's kingdom and doing good. Many of the people believed, and confessed their belief; and in time these became a multitude. Indeed there was a likelihood that by and by all the nation would come into the fold, for the miracles wrought were marvelous, and men found themselves unable to resist such evidences. But after a while there came a day when murmurings began to be heard, and dissatisfaction to show its head. And the cause of this was the very same cause which had worked the opposite effect, previously,—namely, the miracles. The first notable instance was on this wise:

One of the twelve disciples—the same being that Talmage heretofore referred to—was tarrying for a time in Tumblinsonville, healing the sick and teaching in the public places of the village. It was summer, and all the land was parched with a drouth which had lasted during three months. The usual petitions had been offered up, daily at the hearth-stone and on Sundays from the pulpit, but without result—the rain did not come. The governor finally issued his proclamation for a season of fasting and united prayer for rain, naming a certain Sunday for the beginning. St. Talmage sat with the congregation in the Tumblinsonville church that Sunday morning. There was not a cloud in the sky; it was blistering hot; everybody was sad; the preacher said, mournfully, that it was now plain that the rain was withheld for a punishment, and it would be wisest to ask for it no more for the present. At that moment the saint rose up and rebuked the minister before the whole wondering assemblage, for his weak and faltering faith; then he put his two hands together, lifted up his face, and began to pray for rain. With his third sentence an instant darkness came, and with it a pouring deluge! Perhaps one may imagine the faces of the people—it is a thing which cannot be described. The blessed rain continued to come down in torrents all day long, and the happy people talked of nothing but the miracle. Indeed, they were so absorbed in it that it was midnight before they woke up to a sense of the fact that this rain, which began as a blessing, had gradually turned into a calamity—the country was flooded, the whole region was well nigh afloat. Everybody turned out and tried to save cattle, hogs, and bridges; and at this work they wrought despairingly and uselessly two or three hours before it occurred to anybody that *if* that disciple's prayer had brought the deluge, possibly another prayer from him might stop it. Some hurried away and called up the disciple out of his bed, and begged him to stay the flood if he could. He told them to cease from their terrors and bear witness to what was about to happen. He then knelt and offered up his petition. The answer was instantaneous; the rain stopped immediately and utterly.

There was rejoicing in all religious hearts, because the unbelieving had always scoffed at prayer and said the pulpit had claimed that it could accomplish everything, whereas none could prove that it was able to accomplish anything at all. Unbelievers had scoffed when prayers were offered up for better weather, and for the healing of the sick, and the staying of epidemics, and the averting of war—prayers which no living man had ever seen answered, they said. But the holy disciple had shown, now, that special providences were at the bidding of the prayers of the perfect. The evidence was beyond dispute.

But on the other hand there was a widespread discontent among such of the community as had had their all swept away by the flood. It was a feeling which was destined to find a place, later, in other bosoms.

When but a few days had gone by, certain believers came and touched the hem of the disciple's garment and begged that once more he would exert his miraculous powers in the name of Him whom he and they served and worshiped. They desired him to pray for cold weather, for the benefit of a poor widow who was perishing of a wasting fever. He consented; and although it was midsummer, ice formed, and there was a heavy fall of snow. The woman immediately recovered. The destruction of crops by the cold and snow was complete; in addition, a great many persons who were abroad and out of the way of help had their ears and fingers frostbitten, and six children and two old men fell by the wayside, being benumbed by the cold and confused and blinded by the snow, and were frozen to death. Wherefore, although numbers praised God for the miracle, and marveled at it, the relatives and immediate friends of the injured and the killed were secretly discontented, and some of them even gave voice to murmurs.

Now came divers of the elect, praising God, and asked for further changes of the weather, for one reason or another, and the holy disciple, glad to magnify his Lord, willingly gratified them. The calls became incessant. As a consequence, he changed the weather many times, every day. These changes were very trying to the general public, and caused much sickness and death, since alternate drenchings and freezings and scorchings were common, and none could escape colds, in consequence, neither could any ever know, upon going out, whether to wear muslin or furs. A man who dealt in matters of science and had long had a reputation as a singularly accurate weather prophet, found himself utterly baffled by this extraordinary confusion of weather; and his business being ruined, he presently lost his reason and endeavored to take the life of the holy disciple. Eventually so much complaint was made that the saint was induced, by a general petition, to desist, and leave the weather alone. Yet there were many that protested, and were not able to see why they should not be allowed to have prayers offered up for weather to suit their private interests—a thing, they said, which had been done in all ages, and been encouraged by the pulpit, too, until now, when such prayers were found to be worth something. There was a degree of reasonableness in the argument, but it plainly would not answer to listen to it.

An exceedingly sickly season followed the confused and untimely weather, and every house became a hospital. The holy Talmage was urged to interfere with prayer. He did so. The sickness immediately disappeared, and no one was unwell in the slightest degree, during three months. Then the physicians, undertakers and professional nurses of all the region round about rose in a body and made such an outcry that the saint was forced to modify the state of things. He agreed to pray in behalf of special cases, only. Now a young man presently fell sick, and when he was dying his mother begged hard for his life, and the saint yielded, and by his prayers restored him to immediate health. The next day he killed a comrade in a quarrel, and shortly was hanged for it.

His mother never forgave herself for procuring the plans of God to be altered. By request of another mother, another dying son was prayed back to health, but it was not a fortunate thing; for he strangely forsook his blameless ways, and in a few months was in a felon's cell for robbing his employer, and his family were broken hearted and longing for death.

By this time the miracles of the Savior himself were beginning to fall under criticism. He had raised many poor people from the dead; and as long as he had confined himself to the poor these miracles brought large harvests of glory and converts, and nobody found fault, or even thought of finding fault. But a change came at last. A rich bachelor died in a neighboring town, leaving a will giving all his property to the Society for the Encouragement of Missions. Several days after the burial, an absent friend arrived home, and learning of the death, came to Black Jack, and prevailed with the Savior to pray him back to life and health. So the man was alive again, but found himself a beggar; the Society had possession of all his wealth and legal counsel warned the officers of the Society that if they gave it up they would be transcending their powers and the Society could come on them for damages in the full amount, and they would unquestionably be obliged to pay. The officers started to say something about Lazarus, but the lawyer said that if Lazarus left any property behind him he most certainly found himself penniless when he was raised from the dead; that if there was any dispute between him and his heirs, the law upheld the latter. Naturally, the Society decided to hold on to the man's property. There was an aggravating lawsuit; the Society proved that the man had been dead and been buried; the court dismissed the case, saying it could not consider the complaints of a corpse. The matter was appealed; the higher court sustained the lower one. It went further, and said that for a dead man to bring a suit was a thing without precedent, a violation of privilege, and hence was plainly contempt of court—whereupon it laid a heavy fine upon the transgressor. Maddened by these misfortunes, the plaintiff killed the presiding officer of the Society and then blew his own brains out, previously giving warning that if he was disturbed again he would make it a serious matter for the disturber.

The Twelve Disciples were the constant though innocent cause of trouble. Every blessing they brought down upon an individual was sure to fetch curses in its train for other people. Gradually the several communities among whom they labored grew anxious and uneasy; these prayers had unsettled everything; they had so disturbed the order of nature, that nobody could any longer guess, one day, what was likely to happen the next. So the popularity of the Twelve wasted gradually away. The people murmured against them, and said they were a pestilent incumbrance and a dangerous power to have in the State. During the time that they meddled with the weather, they made just one friend every time they changed it, and not less than a hundred enemies—a thing which was natural, and to be expected.—When they agreed to let the weather and the public health alone, their popularity seemed regained, for a while, but they soon lost it once more, through indiscretions. To accommodate a procession, they prayed that the river might be divided; this prayer was answered, and the procession passed over dry-shod. The march consumed twenty minutes, only, but twenty minutes was ample time to enable the backed-up waters to overflow all the country for more than a hundred and fifty miles up the river, on both sides; in consequence of which a vast number of farms and villages were ruined, many lives were lost, immense aggregations of live stock destroyed, and thousands of people reduced to beggary. The disciples had to be spirited away and kept concealed for two or three months, after that, so bitter was the feeling against them, and so widespread the desire to poison or hang them.

In the course of time so many restrictions came to be placed upon the disciples' prayers, by public demand, that they were at last confined to two things, raising the dead and restoring the dying to health. Yet at times even these services produced trouble, and sometimes as great in degree as in the case of the rich bachelor who was raised by the Savior. A very rich old man, with a host of needy kin, was snatched from the very jaws of death by the disciples, and given a long lease of life. The needy kin were not slow to deliver their opinions about what they termed "this outrage"; neither were they mild or measured in their abuse of the holy Twelve. Almost every time a particularly disagreeable person died, his relatives had the annoyance of seeing him walk into their midst again within a week. Often, when such a person was about to die, half the village would be in an anxious and uncomfortable state, dreading the interference of the disciples, each individual hoping they would let nature take its course but none being willing to assume the exceedingly delicate office of suggesting it.

However, a time came at last when people were forced to speak. The region had been cursed, for many years, by the presence of a brute named Marvin, who was a thief, liar, drunkard, blackguard, incendiary, a loathsome and hateful creature in every way. One day the news went about that he was dying. The public joy was hardly concealed. Everybody thought of the disciples in a moment, (for they would be sure to raise him up in the hope of reforming him,) but it was too late. A dozen men started in the direction of Marvin's house, meaning to stand guard there and keep the disciples away; but they were too late; the prayer had been offered, and they met Marvin himself, striding down the street, hale and hearty, and good for thirty years more.

An indignation meeting was called, and there was a packed attendance. It was difficult to maintain order, so excited were the people. Intemperate speeches were made, and resolutions offered in which the disciples were bitterly denounced. Among the resolutions finally adopted were these:

*Resolved*, That the promise "Ask and ye shall receive" shall henceforth be accepted as sound in theory, and true; but it shall stop there; whosoever ventures to actually follow the admonition shall suffer death.

*Resolved*, That to pray for the restoration of the sick; for the averting of war; for the blessing of rain; and for other special providences, were things righteous and admissible whilst they were mere forms and yielded no effect; but henceforth, whosoever shall so pray shall be deemed guilty of crime and shall suffer death.

*Resolved*, That if the ordinary prayers of a nation were answered during a single day, the universal misery, misfortune, destruction and desolation which would ensue, would constitute a cataclysm which would take its place side by side with the deluge and so remain in history to the end of time.

*Resolved*, That whosoever shall utter his belief in special providences in answer to prayer, shall be adjudged insane and shall be confined.

*Resolved*, That the Supreme Being is able to conduct the affairs of this world without the assistance of any person in Arkansas; and whosoever shall venture to offer such assistance shall suffer death.

*Resolved*, That since no one can improve the Creator's plans by procuring their alteration, there shall be but one form of prayer allowed in Arkansas henceforth, and that form shall begin and end with the words, "*Lord, Thy will, not mine, be done*";[5] and whosoever shall add to or take from this prayer, shall perish at the stake.

During several weeks the holy disciples observed these laws, and things moved along, in nature, in a smooth and orderly way which filled the hearts of the harassed people with the deepest gratitude; but at last the Twelve made the sun and moon stand still ten or twelve hours once, to accommodate a sheriff's posse who were trying to exterminate a troublesome band of tramps. The result was frightful. The tides of the ocean being released from the moon's control, burst in one mighty assault upon the shores of all the continents and islands of the globe and swept millions of human beings to instant death. The Savior and the disciples, being warned by friends, fled to the woods, but they were hunted down, one after the other, by the maddened populace, and crucified. With the exception of St. Talmage. For services rendered the detectives, he was paid thirty pieces of silver and his life spared. Thus ended the Second Advent, a.d. 1881.

## NOTES

1. Prior to becoming a state in 1907, Oklahoma comprised a part of the region known as Indian Territory.

2. Horace Greeley (1811–1872), editor of the *New York Tribune* (1841–72) and a founder of the Republican party. James Gordon Bennett (1795–1872), founder and editor of the *New York Herald* (1835–67). Beach is unidentified.

3. See note 1 to "About Smells."

4. Mt. Pelion and Mt. Ossa are two mountains in Greece. In Greek myth, two giants attempted to scale Mt. Olympus by piling the two mountains upon each other, but were killed by Apollo. The phrase "to pile Pelion on Ossa" generally means to attempt a fruitless task, but Twain uses it to suggest the impressiveness of the evidence for Nancy's virgin birth.

5. "Thy will be done in earth, as it is in heaven" (Matt. 6:10; cf. Luke 11:2).

# THE CHARACTER OF MAN
## (1885)

*C*oncerning Man—he is too large a subject to be treated as a whole; so I will merely discuss a detail or two of him at this time. I desire to contemplate him from this point of view—this premiss: that he was not made for any useful purpose, for the reason that he hasn't served any; that he was most likely not even made *intentionally*; and that his working himself up out of the oyster bed to his present position was probably matter of surprise and regret to the Creator; that if he *was* made intentionally, it was not that he might be saved or damned, since he is conspicuously not worth that trouble, but was more probably merely intended as an annoyance—a thing to do for the Creator the office which other vermin do for *us*. If that is really what he was made for his creation does seem rational, explicable, even excusable, in a measure—for the office fits his bulk and his merit. For his history, in all climes, all ages and all circumstances, furnishes oceans and continents of proof that of all the creatures that were made he is the most detestable. Of the entire brood he is the only one— the solitary one—that possesses malice. That is the basest of all instincts, passions, vices—the most hateful. That one thing puts him below the rats, the grubs, the trichinæ. He is the only creature that inflicts pain for sport, knowing it to be pain. But if the cat knows she is inflicting pain when she plays with the frightened mouse, then we must make an exception here; we must grant that in one detail man is the moral peer of the cat. *All* creatures kill—there seems to be no exception; but of the whole list, man is the only one that kills for fun; he is the only one that kills in malice, the only one that kills for revenge. Also—in all the list he is the only creature that has a nasty mind.

Shall he be extolled for his noble qualities, for his gentleness, his sweetness, his amiability, his lovingness, his courage, his devotion, his patience, his fortitude, his prudence, the various charms and graces of his spirit? The other animals share *all* these with him, yet are free from the blacknesses and rottennesses of his character.

Upon what quality, what pretext, then, shall he arrogate to himself the position of the Deity's chosen creature?—His intellect? Will *that* enable him to adorn heaven? It is like the strained wisdom of discarding gas and electricity to pile decayed corpses in the family circle for the sake of the phosphorescent light that issues from them.

Is it free will? He hasn't any more free will than the other creatures.

He has the disposition to do mean and vicious things—and he restrains himself from doing them. Does that make him choicer company for the blest than the lamb, the calf, the horse, the bug that *hasn't* any such disposition? Look at him as you may, there is no rational argument in his favor. Yet he blandly shoves himself forward as the pet of the Deity—the Deity's chosen aimal. We should not forget that the Deity has been accused of picking out the Jews for his favorite people. Those who know that race, know how wanton was that charge. This should make us modester; it should guard us from too readily jumping to gushy and grotesque conclusions from fantastic and irrational premises.

Take one detail. Sham? or "Nature."

There are certain sweet-smelling sugar-coated lies current in the world which all politic men have apparently tacitly conspired together to support and perpetuate. One of these is, that there is such a thing in the world as independence: independence of thought, independence of opinion, independence of action. Another is, that the world loves to *see* independence—admires it, applauds it. Another is, that there is such a thing in the world as toleration—in religion, in politics, and such matters; and with it trains that already mentioned auxiliary lie that toleration is admired, and applauded. One of these trunk-lies spring many branch ones: to-wit, the lie that not all men are slaves; the lie that men are glad when other men succeed; glad when they prosper; glad to see them reach lofty heights; sorry to see them fall again. And yet other branch-lies: to-wit, that there is heroism in man; that he is not mainly made up of malice and treachery; that he is sometimes not a coward; that there is something about him that ought to be perpetuated—in heaven, or hell, or somewhere. And these other branch-lies, to-wit: that conscience, man's moral medicine chest, is not only created by the Creator, but is put into man ready-charged with the right and only true and authentic correctives of conduct—and the duplicate chest, with the self-same correctives, unchanged, unmodified, distributed to all nations and all epochs. And yet one other branch-lie, to-wit, that I am I, and you are you; that we are units, individuals, and have natures of our own, instead of being the tail-end of a tape-worm eternity of ancestors extending in linked procession back—and back—and back—to our source in the monkeys, with this so-called individuality of ours a decayed and rancid mush of inherited instincts and teachings derived, atom by atom, stench by stench, from the entire line of that sorry column, and not so much new and original matter in it as you could balance on a needle point and examine under a microscope. This makes well nigh fantastic the suggestion that there can be such a thing as a personal, original and responsible nature in a man, separable from that in him which is not original, and findable in such quantity as to enable the observer to say, This is a man, not a procession.

Consider that first mentioned lie: that there is such a thing in the world as independence; that it exists in individuals, that it exists in bodies of men. Surely if anything *is* proven, by whole oceans and continents of evidence, it is that the quality of independence was almost wholly left out of the human race. The scattering exceptions to the rule only emphasize it, light it up, make it glare. The whole population of New England meekly took their turns, for years, in standing up in the railway trains, without so much as a complaint above their breath, till at last these uncounted millions were able to produce exactly one single independent man, who stood to his rights and made the railroad give him a seat. Statistics and the law of probabilities warrant the assumption that it will take New England forty years to breed his fellow. There is a law, with a penalty attached, for-bidding trains to occupy the Asylum street crossing more than five minutes at a time. For years people and carriages used to wait there nightly as much as twenty minutes on a stretch while New England trains monopolized that crossing. I used to hear men use vigorous language about that insolent wrong—but they waited, just the same.

We are discreet sheep; we wait to see how the drove is going, and then go with the drove. We have two opinions: one private, which we are afraid to express; and one—the one we use—which we force ourselves to wear to please Mrs. Grundy, until habit makes us comfortable in it, and the custom of defending it presently makes us love it, adore it, and forget how pitifully we came by it. Look at it in politics. Look at the candidates whom we loathe, one year, and are afraid to vote against the next, whom we cover with unimaginable filth, one year, and fall down on the public platform and worship, the next—and keep on doing it until the habitual shutting of our eyes to last year's evidences brings us presently to a sincere and stupid belief in this year's.[1] Look at the tyranny of party—at what is called party allegiance, party loyalty—a snare invented by designing men for selfish purposes—and which turns voters into chattels, slaves, rabbits; and all the while, their masters, and they themselves are shouting rubbish about liberty, independence, freedom of opinion, freedom of speech, honestly unconscious of the fantastic contradiction; and forgetting or ignoring that their fathers and the churches shouted the same blasphemies a generation earlier when thet were closing their doors against the hunted slave, beating his handful of humane defenders with Bible-texts and billies, and pocketing the insults and licking the shoes of his Southern master.

If we would learn what the human race really *is*, at bottom, we need only observe it in election times. A Hartford clergyman met me in the street, and spoke of a new nominee—denounced the nomination, in strong, earnest words—words that were refreshing for their independence, their manliness.[2] He said, "I ought to be proud, perhaps, for this nominee is a relative of mine; on the contrary I am humiliated and disgusted; for I know him intimately—familiarly—and I know that he is an unscrupulous scoundrel, and always has been." You should have seen this clergyman preside at a political meeting forty days later; and urge, and plead, and gush—and you should have heard him paint the character of this same nominee. You would have supposed he was describing the Cid, and Great-heart, and Sir Galahad, and Bayard the Spotless all rolled into one. Was he sincere? Yes—by that time; and therein lies the pathos of it all, the hopelessness of it all. It shows at what trivial cost of effort a man can teach himself a lie, and learn to believe it, when he perceives, by the general drift, that that is the popular thing to do. Does he believe his lie *yet?* Oh, probably not; he has no further use for it. It was but a passing incident; he spared to it the moment that was its due, then hastened back to the serious business of his life.

And what a paltry poor lie is that one which teaches that independence of action and opinion is prized in men, admired, honored, rewarded. When a man leaves a political party, he is treated as if the party owned him—as if he were its bond slave, as most party men plainly are—and had stolen himself, gone off with what was not his own. And he is traduced, derided, despised, held up to public obloquy and loathing. His character is remorselessly assassinated; no means, however vile, are spared to injure his property and his business. If I may speak personally, take my own case. A year ago I had a friend in every newspaper in the land, and a reputation which was worth almost any commonplace man's having. I cast a vote for conscience' sake, and now if anybody values my reputation it is not I.

The preacher who casts a vote for conscience' sake, runs the risk of starving. And is rightly served; for he has been teaching a falsity—that men respect and honor independence of thought and action.

Mr. Beecher[3] may be charged with a *crime*, and his whole following will rise as one man, and stand by him to the bitter end; but who so poor to be his friend when he is charged with casting a vote for conscience' sake? Take the editor so charged—take—take anybody.

All the talk about tolerance, in anything or anywhere, is plainly a gentle lie. It does not exist. It is in no man's heart; but it unconsciously and by moss-grown inherited habit, drivels and slobbers from all men's lips. Intolerance is everything for one's self, and nothing for the other person. The mainspring of man's nature is just that—selfishness. What a fine irony it was to devise the Christian religion for such as he with its golden array of impossibilities: Give *all* thou hast to the poor;[4] if a man smite thee on thy right cheek;[5] if a man borrow thy coat of thee;[6] if a man require thee to go with him a mile;[7] do unto others as you would that others should do unto you;[8] love thy neighbor as thyself.[9] It has supplanted the old religion which went before it—upon men's lips it has.

But not in their hearts. That old religion knew men better than this one, and must outlive it: for it says, "Smite those people hip and thigh; burn all they possess with fire; kill the cattle; kill the old men, and the women, and the young children, and the sucklings; spare nothing that has life; for their opinions are not like ours."

Let us skip the other lies, for brevity's sake. To consider them would prove nothing, except that man is what he is—loving, toward his own, lovable, to his own,—his family, his friends—and, otherwise the buzzing, busy, trivial, enemy of his race—who tarries his little day, does his little dirt, commends himself to God, and then goes out into the darkness, to return no more, and send no messages back—selfish even in death.

## NOTES

1. *Jan. 11, '06.* It is long ago, but it plainly means Blaine. [MT] [For Blaine, see note 18 to "What Is Man?"]

2. *Jan. 11, '06.* I can't remember his name. It began with K, I think. He was one of the American revisers of the New Testament, and was nearly as great a scholar as Hammond Trumbull. [MT] [Hammond Trumbull (1821–1897), Connecticut historian who focused on the languages of the local Native American tribes.]

3. Henry Ward Beecher (1813–1881), renowned Presbyterian minister and writer who became embroiled in a notorious adultery trial in which he was found innocent chiefly by reason of his exalted reputation.

4. Matt. 19:21; Mark 10:21; Luke 18:22.

5. Matt. 5:39.

6. Twain seems to be conflating two passages: "And if any man will sue thee at the law, and take away thy coat, let him have thy cloak also" (Matt. 5:40; cf. Luke 6:29); "Give to him that asketh thee, and from him that would borrow of thee turn thou not away" (Matt. 5:42).

7. Matt. 5:41.

8. Matt. 7:12.

9. Matt. 22:39; Mark 12:31; Luke 10:27.

# LETTER FROM THE RECORDING ANGEL
## (ca. 1885)

Office of the Recording Angel,
Dept. of Petitions, Jan. 20.
Andrew Langdon,[1]
Coal Dealer, Buffalo, N. Y.

I have the honor, as per command, to inform you that your recent act of benevolence and self-sacrifice has been recorded upon a page by itself of the Book called Golden Deeds of Men; a distinction, I am permitted to remark, which is not merely extraordinary, it is unique.

As regards your prayers, for the week ending the 19th, I have the honor to report as follows:

1. For weather to advance hard coal 15 cents per ton. Granted.
2. For influx of laborers to reduce wages 10 per cent. Granted.
3. For a break in rival soft-coal prices. Granted.
4. For a visitation upon the man, or upon the family of the man, who has set up a competing retail coal-yard in Rochester. Granted, as follows: diphtheria, 2, 1 fatal; scarlet fever, 1, to result in deafness and imbecility. Note. This prayer should have been directed against this subordinate's principals, the N. Y. Central RR Co.
5. For deportation to Sheol, of annoying swarms of persons who apply daily for work, or for favors of one sort or another. Taken under advisement for later decision and compromise, this petition appearing to conflict with another one of same date, which will be cited further along.
6. For application of some form of violent death to neighbor who threw brick at family cat, whilst the which was serenading. Reserved for consideration and compromise, because of conflict with a prayer of even date to be cited further along.

7. To "damn the missionary cause." Reserved also—as above.

8. To increase December profits of $22,230 to $45,000 for January, and perpetuate a proportionate monthly increase thereafter— "which will satisfy you." The prayer granted; the added remark accepted with reservations.

9. For cyclone, to destroy the works and fill up the mine of the North Pennsylvania Co. Note: Cyclones are not kept in stock in the winter season. A reliable article of fire-damp can be furnished upon application.

Especial note is made of the above list, they being of particular moment. The 298 remaining supplications classifiable under the head of Special Providences, Schedule A, for week ending 19th, are granted in a body, except that 3 of the 32 cases requiring immediate death have been modified to incurable disease.

This completes the week's invoice of petitions known to this office under the technical designation of Secret Supplications of the Heart, and which for a reason which may suggest itself, always receive our first and especial attention.

The remainder of the week's invoice falls under the head of what we term Public Prayers, in which classification we place prayers uttered in Prayer Meeting, Sunday School, Class Meeting, Family Worship, etc. These kinds of prayers have value according to classification of Christian uttering them. By rule of this office, Christians are divided into two grand classes, to-wit: 1, Professing Christians; 2, Professional Christians. These, in turn, are minutely subdivided and classified by Size, Species, and Family; and finally, Standing is determined by carats, the minimum being 1, the maximum 1,000.

As per balance-sheet for quarter ending Dec. 31st, 1847, you stood classified as follows:

*Grand Classification*, Professing Christian.
*Size*, one-fourth of maximum.
*Species*, Human-Spiritual.

*Family*, A of the Elect, Division 16.
*Standing*, 322 carats fine.

As per balance-sheet for quarter just ended,—that is to say, forty years later,—you stand classified as follows:

*Grand Classification*, Professional Christian.
*Size*, six one-hundredths of maximum.
*Species*, Human-Animal.
*Family*, W of the Elect, Division 1547.
*Standing*, 3 carats fine.

I have the honor to call your attention to the fact that you seem to have deteriorated.

To resume report upon your Public Prayers—with the side remark that in order to encourage Christians of your grade and of approximate grades, it is the custom of this office to grant many things to them which would not be granted to Christians of a higher grade—partly because they would not be asked for:

Prayer for weather mercifully tempered to the needs of the poor and the naked. Denied. This was a Prayer-Meeting prayer. It conflicts with Item 1 of this Report, which was a Secret Supplication of the Heart. By a rigid rule of this office, certain sorts of Public Prayers of Professional Christians are forbidden to take precedence of Secret Supplications of the Heart.

Prayer for better times and plentier food "for the hard handed son of toil whose patient and exhausting labors make comfortable the homes, and pleasant the ways, of the more fortunate, and entitle him to our vigilant and effective protection from the wrongs and injustices which grasping avarice would do him, and to the tenderest offices of our grateful hearts." Prayer-Meeting Prayer. Refused. Conflicts with Secret Supplication of the Heart No. 2.

Prayer "that such as in any way obstruct our preferences may be generously blessed, both themselves and their families, we here calling our hearts to witness that in their worldly prosperity we are spiritually blessed, and our joys made perfect." Prayer-Meeting Prayer. Refused. Conflicts with Secret Supplications of the Heart Nos. 3 and 4.

"Oh, let none fall heir to the pains of perdition through words or acts of ours." Family Worship. Received fifteen minutes in advance of Secret Supplication of the Heart No. 5, with which it distinctly conflicts. It is suggested that one or the other of these prayers be withdrawn, or both of them modified.

"Be mercifully inclined toward all who would do us offence in our persons or our property." Includes man who threw brick at cat. Family Prayer. Received some minutes in advance of No. 6, Secret Supplications of the Heart. Modification suggested, to reconcile discrepancy.

"Grant that the noble missionary cause, the most precious labor entrusted to the hands of men, may spread and prosper without let or limit in all heathen lands that do as yet reproach us with their spiritual darkness." Uninvited prayer shoved in at meeting of American Board. Received nearly half a day in advance of No. 7, Secret Supplications of the Heart. This office takes no stock in missionaries, and is not connected in any way with the American Board. We should like to grant one of these prayers, but cannot grant both. It is suggested that the American Board one be withdrawn.

This office desires for the twentieth time to call urgent attention to your remark appended to No. 8. It is a chestnut.

Of the 464 specifications contained in your Public Prayers for the week, and not previously noted in this report, we grant 2, and deny the rest. To-wit: Granted, (1), "that the clouds may continue to perform their office; (2), and the sun his." It was the divine purpose anyhow; it will gratify you to know that you have not disturbed it. Of the 462 details refused, 61 were uttered in Sunday School. In this connection I must once more remind you that we grant no Sunday School Prayers of Professional Christians of the classification technically known in this office as the John Wanamaker grade.[2] We merely enter them as "words," and they count to his credit according to number uttered within certain limits of time, 3,000 per quarter-minute required, or no score; 4,700 in a possible 5,000 is a quite common Sunday School score, among experts, and counts the same as two hymns and a bouquet furnished by young ladies in the assassin's cell, execution-morning. Your remaining 401 details count for wind only. We bunch them and use them for head-winds in retarding the ships of improper people, but it takes so many of them to make an impression that we cannot allow anything for their use.

I desire to add a word of my own to this report. When certain sorts of people do a sizeable good deed, we credit them up a thousand-fold more for it than we would in the case of a better man—on account of the strain. You stand far away above your classification-record here, because of certain self-sacrifices of yours which greatly exceed what could have been expected of you. Years ago, when you were worth only $100,000, and sent $2 to your impoverished cousin the widow, when she appealed to you for help, there were many in heaven who were not able to believe it, and many more who believed that the money was counterfeit. Your character went up many degrees when it was shown that these suspicions were unfounded. A year or two later, when you sent the poor girl $4 in answer to another appeal, everybody believed it, and you were all the talk here for days together. Two years later you sent $6, upon supplication, when the widow's youngest child died, and that act made perfect your good fame. Everybody in heaven said, "Have you heard about Andrew?"—for you are now affectionately called Andrew here. Your increasing donation, every two or three years, has kept your name on all lips, and warm in all hearts. All heaven watches you Sundays, as you drive to church in your handsome carriage; and when your hand retires from the contribution plate, the glad shout is heard even to the ruddy walls of remote Sheol, "Another nickel from Andrew!" But the climax came a few days ago, when the widow wrote and said she could get a school in a far village to teach if she had $50 to get herself and her two surviving children over the long journey; and you counted up last month's clear profit from your three coal mines—$22,230—and added to it the certain profit for the current month—$45,000 and a possible fifty—and then got down your pen and your check-book and mailed her *fifteen whole dollars!* Ah, Heaven bless and keep you forever and ever, generous heart! There was not a dry eye in the realms of bliss; and amidst the handshakings, and embracings, and praisings, the decree was thundered forth from the shining mount, that this deed should out-honor all the historic self-sacrifices of men and angels, and be recorded by itself upon a page of its own, for that the strain of it upon you had been heavier and bitterer than the strain it costs ten thousand martyrs to yield up their lives at the fiery stake; and all said, "What is the giving up of life, to a noble soul, or to ten thousand noble souls, compared with the giving up of fifteen dollars out of the greedy grip of the meanest white man that ever lived on the face of the earth?"

And it was a true word. And Abraham, weeping, shook out the contents of his bosom and pasted the eloquent label there, "Reserved;" and Peter, weeping, said, "He shall be received with a torchlight procession when he comes;" and then all heaven boomed, and was glad you were going there. And so was hell.

[Signed]
The Recording Angel. [seal.]
By command.

## NOTES

1. Andrew Langdon (1835–1919), first cousin of Twain's wife, Olivia, and a coal operator and banker in the Buffalo area.

2. John Wanamaker (1838–1922), a leading Philadelphia merchant and a prominent lay figure in the Presbyterian church.

# THREE STATEMENTS
# FROM THE 1880S

## I

*I* believe in God the Almighty.

I do not believe He has ever sent a message to man by anybody, or delivered one to him by word of mouth, or made Himself visible to mortal eyes at any time or in any place.

I believe that the Old and New Testaments were imagined and written by man, and that no line in them was authorized by God, much less inspired by Him.

I think the goodness, the justice, and the mercy of God are manifested in His works; I perceive that they are manifested toward me in this life; the logical conclusion is that they will be manifested toward me in the life to come, if there should be one.

I do not believe in special providences. I believe that the universe is governed by strict and immutable laws. If one man's family is swept away by a pestilence and another man's spared, it is only the law working: God is not interfering in that small matter, either against the one man or in favor of the other.

I cannot see how eternal punishment hereafter could accomplish any good end, therefore I am not able to believe in it. To chasten a man in order to perfect him might be reasonable enough; to annihilate him when he shall have proved himself incapable of reaching perfection might be reasonable enough: but to roast him forever for the mere satisfaction of seeing him roast would not be reasonable—even the atrocious God imagined by the Jews would tire of the spectacle eventually.

There may be a hereafter, and there may *not* be. I am wholly indifferent about it. If I am appointed to live again, I feel sure it will be for some more sane and useful purpose than to flounder about for ages in a lake of fire and brimstone for having violated a confusion of ill-defined and contradictory rules said (but not evidenced,) to be of divine institution. If annihilation is to follow death, I shall not be *aware* of the annihilation, and therefore shall not care a straw about it.

I believe that the world's moral laws are the outcome of the world's experience. It needed no God to come down out of heaven to tell men that murder and theft and the other immoralities were bad, both for the individual who commits them and for society which suffers from them.

If I break all these moral laws, I cannot see how I injure God by it, for He is beyond the reach of injury from me—I could as easily injure a planet by throwing mud at it. It seems to me that my mis-conduct could only injure me and other men. I cannot *benefit* God by obeying these moral laws—I could as reasonably benefit the planet by withholding my mud. [Let these sentences be read in the light of the fact that I believe I have received moral laws *only* from man—none whatever from God.] Consequently I do not see why I should either be punished or rewarded hereafter for the deeds I do here.

# II

I would not interfere with any one's religion, either to strengthen it or weaken it. I am not able to believe one's religion can affect his hereafter one way or the other, no matter what that religion may be. But it may easily be a great comfort to him in this life—hence it is a valuable possession to him.

Latter-day Protestantism, by selecting the humaner passages of the Bible, and teaching them to the world, whilst allowing those of a different sort to lie dormant, has produced the highest and purest and best individuals which modem society has known. Thus used, the Bible is the most valuable of books. But the strongly-worded authority for all the religious atrocities of the Middle Ages is still in it, and some day or other it may again become as heavy a curse to the world as it formerly was. The devastating powers of the Book are only suspended, not extinguished. An Expurgated Bible would not be an unuseful thing.

# III

If the very greatest and wisest and most experienced man the earth could produce should write a book, it would be instinct with common sense— it would not totally lack this quality in any clause or sentence. If it made a statement, it would be a statement possible of belief. If it made a requirement, it would be one possible to be obeyed.

If the Bible had been written by God, it also would have possessed these virtues. But it conspicuously lacks them in places. Therefore I think that it not only was not written by God, but was not even written by remarkably capable *men*.

God could have said "Thou shalt not commit adultery";[1] but He would not have followed it up in the same book by plainly violating His own law with Mary the betrothed bride of Joseph. The lamest of modern book-makers would hardly be guilty of so egregious a blunder as that.

To become a right Christian, one must *hate* his brother, his sister, his wife, etc. The laws of God and nature being stronger than those of men, this one must always remain a dead-letter. It was not worth while to cumber the Book with this one, since no single individual of all the earth's myriads would ever be able to obey it.

"Straight is the gate and narrow is the way, and *few there be*,"[2] etc. This is the utterance of the same authority which commands man to "multiply and replenish the earth."[3] What! meekly and obediently proceed to beget children, with the distinct understanding that *nearly all* of them must become fuel for the fires of hell? The person who could obey such a command, under such an understanding, would be simply a monster—no gentler term would describe him. How easily men are self-duped. Many *think* they believe they are begetting fuel for hell, but down in their hearts they believe nothing of the kind.

## NOTES

1. Exod. 20:14.

2. Matt. 7:14. The idea is that few human beings will get to heaven, and most will be consigned to hell.

3. Gen. 1:28, 9:1.

# BIBLE TEACHING AND RELIGIOUS PRACTICE
## (1890)

*R*eligion had its share in the changes of civilization and national character, of course. What share? The lion's. In the history of the human race this has always been the case, will always be the case, to the end of time, no doubt; or at least until man by the slow processes of evolution shall develop into something really fine and high—some billions of years hence, say.

The Christian's Bible is a drugstore. Its contents remain the same; but the medical practice changes. For eighteen hundred years these changes were slight—scarcely noticeable. The practice was allopathic— allopathic in its rudest and crudest form. The dull and ignorant physician day and night, and all the days and all the nights, drenched his patient with vast and hideous doses of the most repulsive drugs to be found in the store's stock; he bled him, cupped him, purged him, puked him, salivated him, never gave his system a chance to rally, nor nature a chance to help. He kept him religion-sick for eighteen centuries, and allowed him not a well day during all that time. The stock in the store was made up of about equal portions of baleful and debilitating poisons, and healing and comforting medicines; but the practice of the time confined the physician to the use of the former; by consequence, he could only damage his patient, and that is what he did.

Not until far within our century was any considerable change in the practice introduced; and then mainly, or in effect only, in Great Britain and the United States. In the other countries today, the patient either still takes the ancient treatment or does not call the physician, at all. In the English-speaking countries the changes observable in our century were forced by that very thing just referred to—the revolt of the patient against the system; they were not projected by the physician. The patient fell to doctoring himself, and the physician's practice began to fall off. He modified his method to get back his trade. He did it gradually, reluctantly; and never yielded more at a time than the pressure compelled. At first he relinquished the daily dose of hell and damnation, and administered it every other day only; next he allowed another day to pass; then another and presently another; when he had restricted it at last to Sundays, and imagined that now there would surely be a truce, the homeopath arrived on the field and made him abandon hell and damnation altogether, and administered Christ's love, and comfort, and charity and compassion in its stead. These had been in the drugstore all the time, gold labeled and conspicuous among the long shelfloads of repulsive purges and vomits and poisons, and so the practice was to blame that they had remained unused, not the pharmacy. To the ecclesiastical physician of fifty years ago, his predecessor for eighteen centuries was a quack; to the ecclesiastical physician of today, his predecessor of fifty years ago was a quack. To the every-man-his-own-ecclesiastical-doctor of—when?—what will the ecclesiastical physician of today be? Unless evolution, which has been a truth ever since the globes, suns, and planets of the solar system were but wandering films of meteor dust, shall reach a limit and become a lie, there is but one fate in store for him.

The methods of the priest and the parson have been very curious, their history is very entertaining. In all the ages the Roman Church has owned slaves, bought and sold slaves, authorized and encouraged her children to trade in them. Long after some Christian peoples had freed their slaves the Church still held on to hers. If any could know, to absolute certainty, that all this was right, and according to God's will and desire, surely it was she, since she was God's specially appointed representative in the earth and sole authorized and infallible expounder of his Bible. There were the texts; there was no mistaking their meaning; she was right, she was doing in this thing what the Bible had mapped out for her to do. So unassailable was her position that in all the centuries she had no word to say against human slavery. Yet now at last, in our immediate day, we hear a Pope saying slave trading is wrong, and we see him sending an expedition to Africa to stop it. The texts remain: it is the practice that has changed. Why? Because the world has corrected the Bible. The Church never corrects it; and also never fails to drop in at the tail of the procession—and take the credit of the correction. As she will presently do in this instance.

Christian England supported slavery and encouraged it for two hundred and fifty years, and her Church's consecrated ministers looked on, sometimes taking an active hand, the rest of the time indifferent. England's interest in the business may be called a Christian interest, a Christian industry. She had her full share in its revival after a long period of inactivity, and this revival was a Christian monopoly; that is to say, it was in the hands of Christian countries exclusively. English parliaments aided the slave traffic and protected it; two English kings held stock in slave-catching companies. The first regular English slave hunter—John Hawkins,[1] of still revered memory—made such successful havoc on his second voyage, in the matter of surprising and burning villages, and maiming, slaughtering, capturing, and selling their unoffending inhabitants, that his delighted queen conferred the chivalric honor of knighthood on him—a rank which had acquired its chief esteem and distinction in other and earlier fields of Christian effort. The new knight, with characteristic English frankness and brusque simplicity, chose as his device the figure of a Negro slave, kneeling and in chains. Sir John's work was the invention of Christians, was to remain a bloody and awful monopoly in the hands of Christians for a quarter of a millennium, was to destroy homes, separate families, enslave friendless men and women, and break a myriad of human hearts, to the end that Christian nations might be prosperous and comfortable, Christian churches be built, and the gospel of the meek and merciful Redeemer be spread abroad in the earth; and so in the name of his ship, unsuspected but eloquent and clear, lay hidden prophecy. She was called *The Jesus.*

But at last in England, an illegitimate Christian rose against slavery. It is curious that when a Christian rises against a rooted wrong at all, he is usually an illegitimate Christian, member of some despised and bastard sect. There was a bitter struggle, but in the end the slave trade had to go—and went. The Biblical authorization remained, but the practice changed.

Then—the usual thing happened; the visiting English critic among us began straightway to hold up his pious hands in horror at our slavery. His distress was unappeasable, his words full of bitterness and contempt. It is true we had not so many as fifteen hundred thousand slaves for him to worry about, while his England still owned twelve millions, in her foreign possessions; but that fact did not modify his wail any, or stay his tears, or soften his censure. The fact that every time we had tried to get rid of our slavery in previous generations, but had always been obstructed, balked, and defeated by England, was a matter of no consequence to him; it was ancient history, and not worth the telling.

Our own conversion came at last. We began to stir against slavery. Hearts grew soft, here, there, and yonder. There was no place in the land where the seeker could not find some small budding sign of pity for the slave. No place in all the land but one—the pulpit. It yielded at last; it always does. It fought a strong and stubborn fight, and then did what it always does, joined the procession—at the tail end. Slavery fell. The slavery text remained; the practice changed, that was all.

During many ages there were witches. The Bible said so. The Bible commanded that they should not be allowed to live.[2] Therefore the Church, after doing its duty in but a lazy and indolent way for eight hundred years, gathered up its halters, thumbscrews, and firebrands, and set about its holy work in earnest. She worked hard at it night and day during nine centuries and imprisoned, tortured, hanged, and burned whole hordes and armies of witches, and washed the Christian world clean with their foul blood.

Then it was discovered that there was no such thing as witches, and never had been. One does not know whether to laugh or to cry. Who discovered that there was no such thing as a witch—the priest, the parson? No, these never discover anything. At Salem, the parson clung pathetically to his witch text after the laity had abandoned it in remorse and tears for the crimes and cruelties it had persuaded them to do. The parson wanted more blood, more shame, more brutalities; it was the unconsecrated laity that stayed his hand. In Scotland the parson killed the witch after the magistrate had pronounced her innocent; and when the merciful legislature proposed to sweep the hideous laws against witches from the statute book, it was the parson who came imploring, with tears and imprecations, that they be suffered to stand.

There are no witches. The witch text remains; only the practice has changed. Hell-fire is gone, but the text remains. Infant damnation is gone, but the text remains. More than two hundred death penalties are gone from the law books, but the texts that authorized them remain.

Is it not well worthy of note that of all the multitude of texts through which man has driven his annihilating pen he has never once made the mistake of obliterating a good and useful one? It does certainly seem to suggest that if man continues in the direction of enlightenment, his religious practice may, in the end, attain some semblance of human decency.

## NOTES

1. Admiral John Hawkins (1532–1595), British shipbuilder and commander, was a pioneer in the British slave trade. On his second voyage, in 1564, on the ship *The Jesus of Lubeck*, Hawkins kidnapped four hundred slaves from Africa and sold them to Spaniards in Colombia, South America.

2. "Thou shalt not suffer a witch to live" (Exod. 22:18).

# MAN'S PLACE IN THE ANIMAL WORLD
## (1896)

In August, 1572, similar things were occurring in Paris and elsewhere in France. In this case it was Christian against Christian. The Roman Catholics, by previous concert, sprung a surprise upon the unprepared and unsuspecting protestants, and butchered them by thousands—both sexes and all ages. This was the memorable St. Bartholomew's Day. At Rome the Pope and the Church gave public thanks to God when the happy news came.

During several centuries hundreds of heretics were burned at the stake every year because their religious opinions were not satisfactory to the Roman Church.

In all ages the savages of all lands have made the slaughtering of their neighboring brothers and the enslaving of their women and children the common business of their lives.

Hypocrisy, envy, malice, cruelty, vengefulness, seduction, rape, robbery, swindling, arson, bigamy, adultery, and the oppression and humiliation of the poor and the helpless in all ways, have been and still are more or less common among both the civilized and uncivilized peoples of the earth.

For many centuries "the common brotherhood of man" has been urged—on Sundays—and "patriotism" on Sundays and week-days both. Yet patriotism *contemplates the opposite of a common brotherhood.*

Woman's equality with man has never been conceded by any people, ancient or modern, civilized or savage.[1]

*I* have been scientifically studying the traits and dispositions of the "lower animals" (so-called,) and contrasting them with the traits and dispositions of man. I find the result profoundly humiliating to me. For it obliges me to renounce my allegiance to the Darwinian theory of the Ascent of Man from the Lower Animals; since it now seems plain to me that that theory ought to be vacated in favor of a new and truer one, this new and truer one to be named the Descent of Man from the Higher Animals.

In proceeding toward this unpleasant conclusion I have not guessed or speculated or conjectured, but have used what is commonly called the scientific method. That is to say, I have subjected every postulate that presented itself, to the crucial test of actual experiment, and have adopted it or rejected it according to the result. Thus I verified and established each step of my course in its turn before advancing to the next. These experiments were made in the London Zöological Gardens, and covered many months of pains-taking and fatiguing work.

Before particularizing any of the experiments, I wish to state one or two things which seem to more properly belong in this place than further along. This in the interest of clearness. The massed experiments established to my satisfaction certain generalizations, to-wit:

1. That the human race is of one distinct species. It exhibits slight variations—in color, stature, mental calibre, and so on—due to climate, environment, and so forth; but it is a species by itself, and not to be confounded with any other.

2. That the quadrupeds are a distinct family, also. This family exhibits variations—in color, size, food-preferences and so on; but it is a faintly by itself.

3. That the other families—the birds, the fishes, the insects, the reptiles, etc., are more or less distinct, also. They are in the procession. They are links in the chain which stretches down from the higher animals to man at the bottom.

Some of my experiments were quite curious. In the course of my reading I had come across a case where, many years ago, some hunters on our Great Plains organized a buffalo hunt for the entertainment of an English earl—that, and to provide some fresh meat for his larder. They had charming sport. They killed seventy-two of those great animals; and ate part of one of them and left the seventy-one to rot. In order to determine the difference between an anaconda and an earl—if any—I caused seven young calves to be turned into the anaconda's cage. The grateful reptile immediately crushed one of them and swallowed it, then lay back satisfied. It showed no further interest in the calves, and no disposition to harm them. I tried this experiment with other anacondas, always with the same result. The fact stood proven that the difference between an earl and an anaconda is, that the earl is cruel and the anaconda isn't; and that the earl wantonly destroys what he has no use for, but the anaconda doesn't. This seemed to suggest that the anaconda was not descended from the earl. It also seemed to suggest that the earl was descended from the anaconda, and had lost a good deal in the transition.

I was aware that many men who have accumulated more millions of money than they can ever use, have shown a rabid hunger for more, and have not scrupled to cheat the ignorant and the helpless out of their poor savings in order to partially appease that appetite. I furnished a hundred different kinds of wild and tame animals the opportunity to accumulate vast stores of food, but none of them would do it. The squirrels and bees and certain birds made accumulations, but stopped when they had gathered a winter's supply, and could not be persuaded to add to it either honestly or by chicane. In order to bolster up a tottering reputation the ant pretended to store up supplies, but I was not deceived. I know the ant. These experiments convinced me that there is this difference between man and the higher animals: he is avaricious and miserly, they are not.

In the course of my experiments I convinced myself that among the animals man is the only one that harbors insults and injuries, broods over them, waits till a chance offers, then takes revenge. The passion of revenge is unknown to the higher animals.

Roosters keep harems, but it is by consent of their concubines; therefore no wrong is done. Men keep harems, but it is by brute force, privileged by atrocious laws which the other sex were allowed no hand in making. In this matter man occupies a far lower place than the rooster.

Cats are loose in their morals, but not consciously so. Man, in his descent from the cat, has brought the cat's looseness with him but has left the unconsciousness behind—the saving grace which excuses the cat. The cat is innocent, man is not.

Indecency, vulgarity, obscenity—these are strictly confined to man; he invented them. Among the higher animals there is no trace of them. They hide nothing; they are not ashamed. Man, with his soiled mind, covers himself. He will not even enter a drawing room with his breast and back naked, so alive is he and his mates to indecent suggestion. Man is "the Animal that Laughs." But so does the monkey, as Mr. Darwin pointed out; and so does the Australian bird that is called the laughing jackass. No—man is the Animal that Blushes. He is the only one that does it—or has occasion to.

At the head of this article we see how "three monks were burnt to death" a few days ago, and a prior "put to death with atrocious cruelty." Do we inquire into the details? No; or we should find out that the prior was subjected to unprintable mutilations. Man—when he is a North American Indian—gouges out his prisoner's eyes; when he is King John, with a nephew to render untroublesome, he uses a red-hot iron;[2] when he is a religious zealot dealing with heretics in the Middle Ages, he skins his capture alive and scatters salt on his back; in the first Richard's time he shuts up a multitude of Jew families in a tower and sets fire to it; in Columbus's time he captures a family of Spanish Jews and—but *that* is not printable—in our day in England a man is fined ten shillings for beating his mother nearly to death with a chair, and another man is fined forty shillings for having four pheasant eggs in his possession without being able to satisfactorily explain how he got them. Of all the animals, man is the only one that is cruel. He is the only one that inflicts pain for the pleasure of doing it. It is a trait that is not known to the higher animals. The cat plays with the frightened mouse; but she has this excuse, that she does not know that the mouse is suffering. The cat is moderate—unhumanly moderate: she only scares the mouse, she does not hurt it, she doesn't dig out its eyes, or tear off its skin, or drive splinters under its nails—man-fashion; when she is done playing with it she makes a sudden meal of it and puts it out of its trouble. Man is the Cruel Animal. He is alone in that distinction.

The higher animals engage in in individual fights, but never in organized masses. Man is the only animal that deals in that atrocity of atrocities, War. He is the only one that gathers his brethren about him and goes forth in cold blood and with calm pulse to exterminate his kind. He is the only animal that for sordid wages will march out, as the Hessians did in our Revolution, and as the boyish Prince Napoleon did in the Zulu war,[3] and help to slaughter strangers of his own species who have done him no harm and with whom he has no quarrel.

Man is the only animal that robs his helpless fellow of his country—takes possession of it and drives him out of it or destroys him. Man has done this in all the ages. There is not an acre of ground on the globe that is in possession of its rightful owner, or that has not been taken away from owner after owner, cycle after cycle, by force and bloodshed.

Man is the only Slave. And he is the only animal who enslaves. He has always been a slave in one form or another, and has always held other slaves in bondage under him in one way or another. In our day he is always some man's slave for wages, and does that man's work; and this slave has other slaves under him for minor wages, and they do *his* work. The higher animals are the only ones who exclusively do their own work and provide their own living.

Man is the only Patriot. He sets himself apart in his own country, under his own flag, and sneers at the other nations, and keeps multitudinous uniformed assassins on hand at heavy expense to grab slices of other people's countries, and *keep* them from grabbing slices of *his*. And in the intervals between campaigns he washes the blood off his hands and works for "the universal brotherhood of man"—with his mouth.

Man is the Religious Animal. He is the only Religious Animal. He is the only animal that has the True Religion—several of them. He is the only animal that loves his neighbor as himself, and cuts his throat if his theology isn't straight. He has made a graveyard of the globe in trying his honest best to smooth his brother's path to happiness and heaven. He was at it in the time of the Caesars, he was at it in Mahomet's time, he was at it in the time of the Inquisition, he was at it in France a couple of centuries, he was at it in England in Mary's day, he has been at it ever since he first saw the light, he is at it to-day in Crete—as per the telegrams quoted above—he will be at it somewhere else to-morrow. The higher animals have no religion. And we are told that they are going to be left out, in the Hereafter. I wonder why? It seems questionable taste.

Man is the Reasoning Animal. Such is the claim. I think it is open to dispute. Indeed, my experiments have proven to me that he is the Unreasoning Animal. Note his history, as sketched above. It seems plain to me that whatever he is he is *not* a reasoning animal. His record is the fantastic record of a maniac. I consider that the strongest count against his intelligence is the fact that with that record back of him he blandly sets himself up as the head animal of the lot; whereas by his own standards he is the bottom one.

In truth, man is incurably foolish. Simple things which the other animals easily learn, he is incapable of learning. Among my experiments was this. In an hour I taught a cat and a dog to be friends. I put them in a cage. In another hour I taught them to be friends with a rabbit. In the course of two days I was able to add a fox, a goose, a squirrel and some doves. Finally a monkey. They lived together in peace; even affectionately.

Next, in another cage I confined an Irish Catholic from Tipperary, and as soon as he seemed tame I added a Scotch Presbyterian from Aberdeen. Next a Turk from Constantinople; a Greek Christian from Crete; an Armenian; a Methodist from the wilds of Arkansaw; a Bhuddist from China; a Brahmin from Benares. Finally, a Salvation Army Colonel from Wapping. Then I stayed away two whole days. When I came back to note results, the cage of Higher Animals was all right, but in the other there was but a chaos of gory odds and ends of turbans and fezzes and plaids and bones and flesh—not a specimen left alive. These Reasoning Animals had disagreed on a theological detail and carried the matter to a Higher Court.

One is obliged to concede that in true loftiness of character, Man cannot claim to approach even the meanest of the Higher Animals. It is plain that he is constitutionally incapable of approaching that altitude; that he is constitutionally afflicted with a Defect which must make such approach forever impossible, for it is manifest that this Defect is permanent in him, indestructible, ineradicable.

I find this Defect to be the Moral Sense. He is the only animal that has it. It is the secret of his degradation. It is the quality *which enables him to do wrong.* It has no other office. It is incapable of performing any other function. It could never have been intended to perform any other. Without it, man could do no wrong. He would rise at once to the level of the Higher Animals.

Since the Moral Sense has but the one office, the one capacity—to enable man to do wrong—it is plainly without value to him. It is as valueless to him as is disease. In fact it manifestly *is* a disease. *Rabies* is bad, but it is not so bad as this disease. Rabies enables a man to do a thing which he could not do when in a healthy state: kill his neighbor with a poisonous bite. No one is the better man for having rabies. The Moral Sense enables a man to do wrong. It enables him to do wrong in a thousand ways. Rabies is an innocent disease, compared to the Moral Sense. No one, then, can be the better man for having the Moral Sense. What, now, do we find the Primal Curse to have been? Plainly what it was in the beginning: the infliction upon man of the Moral Sense; the ability to distinguish good from evil; and with it, necessarily, the ability to *do* evil; for there can be no evil act without the presence of consciousness of it in the doer of it.

And so I find that we have descended and degenerated, from some far ancestor,—some microscopic atom wandering at its pleasure between the mighty horizons of a drop of water. Perchance,—insect by insect, animal by animal, reptile by reptile, down the long highway of smirchless innocence, till we have reached the bottom stage of development—nameable as the Human Being. Below us—nothing. Nothing but the Frenchman.

There is only one possible stage below the Moral Sense; that is the Immoral Sense. The Frenchman has it. Man is but little lower than the angels. This definitely locates him. He is between the angels and the French.

Man seems to be a rickety poor sort of a thing, any way you take him; a kind of British Museum of infirmities and inferiorities. He is always undergoing repairs. A machine that was as unreliable as he is would have no market. On top of his specialty—the Moral Sense—are piled a multitude of minor infirmities; such a multitude, indeed, that one may broadly call them countless. The higher animals get their teeth without pain or inconvenience. Man gets his through months and months of cruel torture; and at a time of life when he is but ill able to bear it. As soon as he has got them they must all be pulled out again, for they were of no value in the first place, not worth the loss of a night's rest. The second set will answer for a while, by being reinforced occasionally with rubber or plugged up with gold; but he will never get a set which can really be depended on till a dentist makes him one. This set will be called "false" teeth—as if he had ever worn any other kind.

In a wild state—a natural state—the Higher Animals have a few diseases; diseases of little consequence; the main one is old age. But man starts in as a child and lives on diseases till the end, as a regular diet. He has mumps, measles, whooping cough, croup, tonsilitis, diphtheria, scarlet fever, almost as a matter of course. Afterward, as he goes along, his life continues to be threatened at every turn: by colds, coughs, asthma, bronchitis, itch, cholera, cancer, consumption, yellow fever, bilious fever, typhus fevers, hay fever, ague, chilblains, piles, inflammation of the entrails, indigestion, toothache, earache, deafness, dumbness, blindness, influenza, chicken pox, cow pox, small pox, liver complaint, constipation, bloody flux, warts, pimples, boils, carbuncles, abscesses, bunions, corns, tumors, fistulas, pneumonia, softening of the brain, melancholia and fifteen other kinds of insanity; dysentery, jaundice, diseases of the heart, the bones, the skin, the scalp, the spleen, the kidneys, the nerves, the brain, the blood; scrofula, paralysis, leprosy, neuralgia, palsy, fits, headache, thirteen kinds of rheumatism, forty-six of gout, and a formidable supply of gross and unprintable disorders of one sort and another. Also—but why continue the list. The mere names of the agents appointed to keep this shackly machine out of repair would hide him from sight if printed on his body in the smallest type known to the founder's art. He is but a basket of festering offal provided for the support and entertainment of swarming armies of bacilli,—armies commissioned to rot him and destroy him, and each army equipped with a special detail of the work. The process of waylaying him, persecuting him, rotting him, killing him, begins with his first breath, and there is no mercy, no pity, no truce till he draws his last one.

Look at the workmanship of him, in certain of its particulars. What are his tonsils for? They perform no useful function; they have no value. They have no business there. They are but a trap. They have but the one office, the one industry: to provide tonsilitis and quinzy and such things for the possessor of them. And what is the vermiform appendix for? It has no value; it cannot perform any useful service. It is but an ambuscaded enemy whose sole interest in life is to lie in wait for stray grape seeds and employ them to breed strangulated hernia. And what are the male's mammals for? For business, they are out of the question; as an ornament, they are a mistake. What is his beard for? It performs no useful function; it is a nuisance and a discomfort; all nations hate it; all nations persecute it with the razor. And because it is a nuisance and a discomfort, Nature never allows the supply of it to fall short, in any man's case, between puberty and the grave. You never see a man bald-headed on his chin. But his hair! It is a graceful ornament, it is a comfort, it is the best of all protections against certain perilous ailments, man prizes it above emeralds and rubies. And because of these things Nature puts it on, half the time, so that it won't stay. Man's sight, smell, hearing, sense of locality—how inferior they are. The condor sees a corpse at five miles; man has no telescope that can do it. The bloodhound follows a scent that is two days old. The robin hears the earth-worm burrowing his course under the ground. The cat, deported in a closed basket, finds its way home again through twenty miles of country which it has never seen.

For style, look at the Bengal tiger—that ideal of grace, beauty, physical perfection, majesty. And then look at Man—that poor thing. He is the Animal of the Wig, the Trepanned Skull, the Ear Trumpet, the Glass Eye, the Pasteboard Nose, the Porcelain Teeth, the Silver Windpipe, the Wooden Leg—a creature that is mended and patched all over, from top to bottom. If he can't get renewals of his brickabrac in the next world, what will he look like?

He has just one stupendous superiority. In his intellect he is supreme. The Higher Animals cannot touch him there. It is curious, it is noteworthy, that no heaven has ever been offered him wherein his one sole superiority was provided with a chance to enjoy itself. Even when he himself has imagined a heaven, he has never made provision in it for intellectual joys. It is a striking omission. It seems a tacit confession that heavens are provided for the Higher Animals alone. This is matter for thought; and for serious thought. And it is full of a grim suggestion: that we are not as important, perhaps, as we had all along supposed we were.

## NOTES

1. The source of this quotation is the London *Daily Telegraph* (August 13, 1896).

2. During the period when John (later King John I of England) was Count of Mortain (1189–99), he waged a constant struggle to dislodge his nephew, Arthur (son of John's brother Richard I), from succeeding to the throne. He was successful in the attempt, becoming king upon Richard's death in 1199.

3. Prince Imperial Louis Napoleon (1856–1879), son of Emperor Napoleon III of France, accompanied British troops during the British expedition to Zululand and was killed in battle.

# THOUGHTS OF GOD
## (early 1900s)

How often we are moved to admit the intelligence exhibited in both the designing and the execution of some of His works. Take the fly, for instance. The planning of the fly was an application of pure intelligence, morals not being concerned. Not one of us could have planned the fly, not one of us could have constructed him; and no one would have considered it wise to try, except under an assumed name. It is believed by some that the fly was introduced to meet a long-felt want. In the course of ages, for some reason or other, there have been millions of these persons, but out of this vast multitude there has not been one who has been willing to explain what the want was. At least satisfactorily. A few have explained that there was need of a creature to remove disease-breeding garbage; but these being then asked to explain what long-felt want the disease-breeding garbage was introduced to supply, they have not been willing to undertake the contract.

There is much inconsistency concerning the fly. In all the ages he has not had a friend, there has never been a person in the earth who could have been persuaded to intervene between him and extermination; yet billions of persons have excused the Hand that made himand this without a blush. Would they have excused a Man in the same circumstances, a man positively known to have invented the fly? On the contrary. For the credit of the race let us believe it would have been all day with that man. Would these persons consider it just to reprobate in a child, with its undeveloped morals, a scandal which they would overlook in the Pope?

When we reflect that the fly was not invented for pastime, but in the way of business; that he was not flung off in a heedless moment and with no object in view but to pass the time, but was the fruit of long and pains-taking labor and calculation, and with a definite and far-reaching purpose in view; that his character and conduct were planned out with cold deliberation; that his career was foreseen and foreordered, and that there was no want which he could supply, we are hopelessly puzzled, we cannot understand the moral lapse that was able to render possible the conceiving and the consummation of this squalid and malevolent creature.

Let us try to think the unthinkable; let us try to imagine a Man of a sort willing to invent the fly; that is to say, a man destitute of feeling; a man willing to wantonly torture and harass and persecute myriads of creatures who had never done him any harm and could not if they wanted to, and—the majority of them—poor dumb things not even aware of his existence. In a word, let us try to imagine a man with so singular and so lumbering a code of morals as this: that it is fair and right to send afflictions upon the *just*—upon the unoffending as well as upon the offending, without discrimination.

If we can imagine such a man, that is the man that could invent the fly, and send him out on his mission and furnish him his orders: "Depart into the uttermost corners of the earth, and diligently do your appointed work. Persecute the sick child; settle upon its eyes, its face, its hands, and gnaw and pester and sting; worry and fret and madden the worn and tired mother who watches by the child, and who humbly prays for mercy and relief with the pathetic faith of the deceived and the unteachable. Settle upon the soldier's festering wounds in field and hospital and drive him frantic while he also prays, and betweentimes curses, with none to listen but you, Fly, who get all the petting and all the protection, without even praying for it. Harry and persecute the forlorn and forsaken wretch who is perishing of the plague, and in his terror and despair praying; bite, sting, feed upon his ulcers, dabble your feet in his rotten blood, gum them thick with plague-germs—feet cunningly designed and perfected for this function ages ago in abe beginning—carry this freight to a hundred tables, among the just and the unjust, the high and the low, and walk over the food and gaum it with filth and death. Visit all; allow no man peace till he get it in the grave; visit and afflict the hard-worked and unoffending horse, mule, ox, ass, pester the patient cow, and all the kindly animals that labor without fair reward here and perish without hope of it hereafter; spare no creature, wild or tame; but wheresoever you find one, make his life a misery, treat him as the innocent deserve; and so please Me and increase My glory Who made the fly."

We hear much about His patience and forbearance and long-suffering; we hear nothing about our own, which much exceeds it. We hear much about His mercy and kindness and goodness—in words—the words of His Book and of His pulpit—and the meek multitude is content with this evidence, such as it is, seeking no further; but whoso searcheth after a concreted sample of it will in time acquire fatigue. There being no instances of it. For what are gilded as mercies are not in any recorded case more than mere common justices, and *due*—due without thanks or compliment. To rescue without personal risk a cripple from a burning house is not a mercy, it is a mere commonplace duty; anybody would do it that could. And not by proxy, either—delegating the work but confiscating the credit for it. If men neglected "God's poor" and "God's stricken and helpless ones" as He does, what would become of them? The answer is to be found in those dark lands where man follows His example and turns his indifferent back upon them: they get no help at all; they cry, and plead and pray in vain, they linger and suffer, and miserably die. If you will look at the matter rationally and without prejudice, the proper place to hunt for the facts of His mercy, is not where man does the mercies and He collects the praise, but in those regions where He has the field to Himself.

It is plain that there is one moral law for heaven and another for the earth. The pulpit assures us that wherever we see suffering and sorrow which we can relieve and do not do it, we sin, heavily. *There was never yet a case of suffering or sorrow which God could not relieve.* Does He sin, then? If He is the Source of Morals He does—certainly nothing can be plainer than that, you will admit. Surely the Source of law cannot violate law and stand unsmirched; surely the judge upon the bench cannot forbid crime and then revel in it himself unreproached. Nevertheless we have this curious spectacle: daily the trained parrot in the pulpit gravely delivers himself of these ironies, which he has acquired at second-hand and adopted without examination, to a trained congregation which accepts them without examination, and neither the speaker nor the hearer laughs at himself. It does seem as if we ought to be humble when we are at a bench-show, and not put on airs of intellectual superiority there.

# "WAS THE WORLD MADE FOR MAN?"
## (1903)

"Alfred Russell Wallace's revival of the theory that this earth is at the centre of the stellar universe, and is the only habitable globe, has aroused great interest in the world."—*Literary Digest*[1]

"For ourselves we do thoroughly believe that man, as he lives just here on this tiny earth, is in essence and possibilities the most sublime existence in all the range of non-divine being—the chief love and delight of God."—*Chicago "Interior"* (Presb.)

*I* seem to be the only scientist and theologian still remaining to be heard from on this important matter of whether the world was made for man or not. I feel that it is time for me to speak.

I stand almost with the others. They believe the world was made for man, I believe it likely that it was made for man; they think there is proof, astronomical mainly, that it was made for man, I think there is evidence only, not proof, that it was made for him. It is too early, yet, to arrange the verdict, the returns are not all in. When they are all in, I think they will show that the world was made for man; but we must not hurry, we must patiently wait till they are all in.

Now as far as we have got, astronomy is on our side. Mr. Wallace has clearly shown this. He has clearly shown two things: that the world was made for man, and that the universe was made for the world—to stiddy it, you know. The astronomy part is settled, and cannot be challenged.

We come now to the geological part. This is the one where the evidence is not all in, yet. It is coming in, hourly, daily, coming in all the time, but naturally it comes with geological carefulness and deliberation, and we must not be impatient, we must not get excited, we must be calm, and wait. To lose our tranquillity will not hurry geology; nothing hurries geology.

It takes a long time to prepare a world for man, such a thing is not done in a day. Some of the great scientists, carefully ciphering the evidences furnished by geology, have arrived at the conviction that our world is prodigiously old, and they may be right, but Lord Kelvin is not of their opinion.[2] He takes a cautious, conservative view, in order to be on the safe side, and feels sure it is not so old as they think. As Lord Kelvin is the highest authority in science now living, I think we must yield to him and accept his view. He does not concede that the world is more than a hundred million years old. He believes it is that old, but not older. Lyell believed that our race was introduced into the world 31,000 years ago,[3] Herbert Spencer makes it 32,000.[4] Lord Kelvin agrees with Spencer.

Very well. According to these figures it took 99,968,000 years to prepare the world for man, impatient as the Creator doubtless was to see him and admire him. But a large enterprise like this has to be conducted warily, pains-takingly, logically. It was foreseen that man would have to have the oyster. Therefore the first preparation was made for the oyster. Very well, you cannot make an oyster out of whole cloth, you must make the oyster's ancestor first. This is not done in a day. You must make a vast variety of invertebrates, to start with—belemnites, trilobites, jebusites, amalekites, and that sort of fry, and put them to soak in a primary sea, and wait and see what will happen. Some will be a disappointment—the belemnites, the ammonites and such; they will be failures, they will die out and become extinct, in the course of the 19,000,000 years covered by the experiment, but all is not lost, for the amalekites will fetch the home-stake; they will develop gradually into encrinites, and stalactites, and blatherskites, and one thing and another as the mighty ages creep on and the Archaean and the Cambrian Periods pile their lofty crags in the primordial seas, and at last the first grand stage in the preparation of the world for man stands completed, the Oyster is done. An oyster has hardly any more reasoning power than a scientist has; and so it is reasonably certain that this one jumped to the conclusion that the nineteen-million years was a preparation for *him;* but that would be just like an oyster, which is the most conceited animal there is, except man. And anyway, this one could not know, at that early date, that he was only an incident in a scheme, and that there was some more to the scheme, yet.

The oyster being achieved, the next thing to be arranged for in the preparation of the world for man, was fish. Fish, and coal—to fry it with. So the Old Silurian seas were opened up to breed the fish in, and at the same time the great work of building Old Red Sandstone mountains 80,000 feet high to cold-storage their fossils in was begun. This latter was quite indispensable, for there would be no end of failures again, no end of extinctions—millions of them—and it would be cheaper and less trouble to can them in the rocks than keep tally of them in a book. One does not build the coal beds and 80,000 feet of perpendicular Old Red Sandstone in a brief time—no, it took twenty million years. In the first place, a coal bed is a slow and troublesome and tiresome thing to construct. You have to grow prodigious forests of tree-ferns and reeds and calamites and such things in a marshy region; then you have to sink them under out of sight and let them rot; then you have to turn the streams on them, so as to bury them under several feet of sediment, and the sediment must have time to harden and turn to rock; next you must grow another forest on top, then sink it and put on another layer of sediment and harden it; then more forest and more rock, layer upon layer, three miles deep—ah, indeed it is a sickening slow job to build a coal-measure and do it right!

So the millions of years drag on; and meantime the fish-culture is lazying along and frazzling out in a way to make a person tired. You have developed ten thousand kinds of fishes from the oyster; and come to look, you have raised nothing but fossils, nothing but extinctions. There is nothing left alive and progressive but a ganoid or two and perhaps half a dozen asteroids. Even the cat wouldn't eat such.

Still, it is no great matter; there is plenty of time, yet, and they will develop into something tasty before man is ready for them. Even a ganoid can be depended on for that, when he is not going to be called on for sixty million years.

The Palaeozoic time-limit having now been reached, it was necessary to begin the next stage in the preparation of the world for man, by opening up the Mesozoic Age and instituting some reptiles. For man would need reptiles. Not to eat, but to develop himself from. This being the most important detail of the scheme, a spacious liberality of time was set apart for it—thirty million years. What wonders followed! From the remaining ganoids and asteroids and alkaloids were developcd by slow and steady and pains-taking culture those stupendous saurians that used to prowl about the steamy world in those remote ages, with their snaky heads reared forty feet in the air and sixty feet of body and tail racing and thrashing after. All gone, now, alas—all extinct, except the little handful of Arkansawrians left stranded and lonely with us here upon this far-flung verge and fringe of time.

Yes, it took thirty million years and twenty million reptiles to get one that would stick long enough to develop into something else and let the scheme proceed to the next step.

Then the Pterodactyl burst upon the world in all his impressive solemnity and grandeur, and all Nature recognized that the Cainozoic threshold was crossed and a new Period open for business, a new stage begun in the preparation of the globe for man. It may be that the Pterodactyl thought the thirty million years had been intended as a preparation for himself, for there was nothing too foolish for a Pterodactyl to imagine, but he was in error, the preparation was for man. Without doubt the Pterodactyl attracted great attention, for even the least observant could see that there was the making of a bird in him. And so it turned out. Also the makings of a mammal, in time. One thing we have to say to his credit, that in the matter of picturesqueness he was the triumph of his Period; he wore wings and had teeth, and was a starchy and wonderful mixture altogether, a kind of long-distance premonitory symptom of Kipling's marine:

> 'E isn't one o' the reg'lar Line,
>      nor 'e isn't one of the crew,
> 'E's a kind of a giddy harumfrodite—
>      soldier an' sailor too![5]

From this time onward for nearly another thirty million years the preparation moved briskly. From the Pterodactyl was developed the bird; from the bird the kangaroo, from the kangaroo the other marsupials; from these the mastodon, the megatherium, the giant sloth, the Irish elk, and all that crowd that you make useful and instructive fossils out of—then came the first great Ice Sheet, and they all retreated before it and crossed over the bridge at Behring's strait and wandered around over Europe and Asia and died. All except a few, to carry on the preparation with. Six Glacial Periods with two million years between Periods chased these poor orphans up and down and about the earth, from weather to weather—from tropic swelter at the poles to Arctic frost at the equator and back again and to and fro, they never knowing what kind of weather was going to turn up next; and if ever they settled down anywhere the whole continent suddenly sank under them without the least notice and they had to trade places with the fishes and scramble off to where the seas had been, and scarcely a dry rag on them; and when there was nothing else doing a volcano would let go and fire them out from wherever they had located. They led this unsettled and irritating life for twenty-five million years, half the time afloat, half the time aground, and always wondering what it was all for, they never suspecting, of course, that it was a preparation for man and had to be done just so or it wouldn't be any proper and harmonious place for him when he arrived.

And at last came the monkey, and anybody could see that man wasn't far off, now. And in truth that was so. The monkey went on developing for close upon 5,000,000 years, and then turned into a man—to all appearances.

Such is the history of it. Man has been here 32,000 years. That it took a hundred million years to prepare the world for him is proof that that is what it was done for. I suppose it is. I dunno. If the Eiffel tower were now representing the world's age, the skin of paint on the pinnacle-knob at its summit would represent man's share of that age; and anybody would perceive that that skin was what the tower was built for. I reckon they would, I dunno.

## NOTES

1. Twain quotes from an anonymous article, "The Universe for Man After All?," *Literary Digest* 26, no. 12 (March 21, 1903): 423, discussing an article by Alfred Russel (not Russell) Wallace, "Man's Place in the Universe" (*Fortnightly Review*, March 1903), an abstract of a book of the same title (1903). Wallace (1823–1913), a British naturalist, had developed a theory of evolution independently of Darwin; but he was also attracted to spiritualism and religion.

2. William Thomson, Lord Kelvin (1824–1907), Scottish mathematician and physicist, published his views on the age of the earth in such papes as "The Age of the Earth as an Abode Fitted for Life" (1899). It has now been ascertained that the earth is more than four billion years old.

3. Sir Charles Lyell (1797–1875), whose *Elements of Geology* (1830) revolutionized the study of geology. His theories about the origin of humanity can be found in *Geological Evidences of the Antiquity of Man* (1863).

4. Herbert Spencer (1820–1903), British philosopher and sociologist. See part III of his *Principles of Biology* (1864–67).

5. Rudyard Kipling, "'Soldier an' Sailor Too,'" ll. 6–7.

# As Concerns Interpreting the Deity
## (1905)

# I

This line of hieroglyphs was for fourteen years the despair of all the scholars who labored over the mysteries of the Rosetta stone:

After five years of study Champollion translated it thus:

> Therefore let the worship of Epiphanes be maintained in all the temples; this upon pain of death.[1]

That was the twenty-fourth translation that had been furnished by scholars. For a time it stood. But only for a time. Then doubts began to assail it and undermine it, and the scholars resumed their labors. Three years of patient work produced eleven new translations; among them, this, by Grünfeldt,[2] was received with considerable favor:

> The horse of Epiphanes shall be maintained at the public expense; this upon pain of death.

But the following rendering, by Gospodin,[3] was received by the learned world with yet greater favor:

> The priest shall explain the wisdom of Epiphanes to all these people, and these shall listen with reverence, upon pain of death.

Seven years followed in which twenty-one fresh and widely varying renderings were scored—none of them quite convincing. But now, at last, came Rawlinson,[4] the youngest of all the scholars, with a translation which was immediately and universally recognized as being the correct version, and his name became famous in a day. So famous, indeed, that even the children were familiar with it; and such a noise did the achievement itself make that not even the noise of the monumental political event of that same year—the flight from Elba[5]—was able to smother it to silence. Rawlinson's version reads as follows:

> Therefore, walk not away from the wisdom of Epiphanes, but turn and follow it; so shall it conduct thee to the temple's peace, and soften for thee the sorrows of life and the pains of death.

Here is another difficult text:

It is demotic—a style of Egyptian writing and a phase of the language which had perished from the knowledge of all men twenty-five hundred years before the Christian era.

Our red Indians have left many records, in the form of pictures, upon our crags and boulders. It has taken our most gifted and painstaking students two centuries to get at the meanings hidden in these pictures; yet there are still two little lines of hieroglyphs among the figures grouped upon the Dighton Rocks[6] which they have not succeeded in interpreting to their satisfaction. These:

The suggested solutions of this riddle are practically innumerable; they would fill a book.

Thus we have infinite trouble in solving man-made mysteries; it is only when we set out to discover the secret of God that our difficulties disappear. It was always so. In antique Roman times it was the custom of the Deity to try to conceal His intentions in the entrails of birds, and this was patiently and hopefully continued century after century, although the attempted concealment never succeeded, in a single recorded instance. The augurs could read entrails as easily as a modern child can read coarse print. Roman history is full of the marvels of interpretation which these extraordinary men performed. These strange and wonderful achievements move our awe and compel our admiration. Those men could pierce to the marrow of a mystery instantly. If the Rosetta-stone idea had been introduced it would have defeated them, but entrails had no embarrassments for them. Entrails have gone out, now—entrails and dreams. It was at last found out that as hiding-places for the divine intentions they were inadequate.

> A part of the wall of Valletri having in former times been struck with thunder, the response of the soothsayers was, that a native of that town would some time or other arrive at supreme power.
>
> —*Bohn's Suetonius*, p. 138[7]

"Some time or other." It looks indefinite, but no matter, it happened, all the same; one needed only to wait, and be patient, and keep watch, then he would find out that the thunder-stroke had Cæsar Augustus in mind, and had come to give notice.

There were other advance-advertisements. One of them appeared just before Cæsar Augustus was born, and was most poetic and touching and romantic in its feelings and aspects. It was a dream. It was dreamed by Cæsar Augustus's mother, and interpreted at the usual rates:

> Atia, before her delivery, dreamed that her bowels stretched to the stars and expanded through the whole circuit of heaven and earth.
>
> —*Suetonius*, p. 139[8]

That was in the augur's line, and furnished him no difficulties, but it would have taken Rawlinson and Champollion fourteen years to make sure of what it meant, because they would have been surprised and dizzy. It would have been too late to be valuable, then, and the bill for service would have been barred by the statute of limitation.

In those old Roman days a gentleman's education was not complete until he had taken a theological course at the seminary and learned how to translate entrails. Cæsar Augustus's education received this final polish. All through his life, whenever he had poultry on the menu he saved the interiors and kept himself informed of the Deity's plans by exercising upon those interiors the arts of augury.

> In his first consulship, while he was observing the auguries, twelve vultures presented themselves, as they had done to Romulus. And when he offered sacrifice, the livers of all the victims were folded inward in the lower part; a circumstance which was regarded by those present who had skill in things of that nature, as an indubitable prognostic of great and wonderful fortune.
>
> —*Suetonius*, p. 141[9]

"Indubitable" is a strong word, but no doubt it was justified, if the livers were really turned that way. In those days chicken livers were strangely and delicately sensitive to coming events, no matter how far off they might be; and they could never keep still, but would curl and squirm like that, particularly when vultures came and showed interest in that approaching great event and in breakfast.

# II

We may now skip eleven hundred and thirty or forty years, which brings us down to enlightened Christian times and the troubled days of King Stephen of England. The augur has had his day and has been long ago forgotten; the priest had fallen heir to his trade.

King Henry is dead; Stephen, that bold and outrageous person, comes flying over from Normandy to steal the throne from Henry's daughter. He accomplished his crime, and Henry of Huntington, a priest of high degree, mourns over it in his Chronicle. The Archbishop of Canterbury consecrated Stephen: "wherefore the Lord visited the Archbishop with the same judgment which he had inflicted upon him who struck Jeremiah the great priest: he died within a year."[10]

Stephen's was the greater offense, but Stephen could wait; not so the Archbishop, apparently.

> The kingdom was a prey to intestine wars; slaughter, fire, and rapine spread ruin throughout the land; cries of distress, horror, and woe rose in every quarter.

That was the result of Stephen's crime. These unspeakable conditions continued during nineteen years. Then Stephen died as comfortably as any man ever did, and was honorably buried. It makes one pity the poor Archbishop, and wish that he, too, could have been let off as leniently. How did Henry of Huntington know that the Archbishop was sent to his grave by judgment of God for consecrating Stephen? He does not explain. Neither does he explain why Stephen was awarded a pleasanter death than he was entitled to, while the aged King Henry, his predecessor, who had ruled England thirty-five years to the people's strongly worded satisfaction, was condemned to close his life in circumstances most distinctly unpleasant, inconvenient, and disagreeable. His was probably the most uninspiring funeral that is set down in history. There is not a detail about it that is attractive. It seems to have been just the funeral for Stephen, and even at this far-distant day it is matter of just regret that by an indiscretion the wrong man got it.

Whenever God punishes a man, Henry of Huntington knows why it was done, and tells us; and his pen is eloquent with admiration; but when a man has earned punishment, and escapes, he does not explain. He is evidently puzzled, but he does not say anything. I think it is often apparent that he is pained by these discrepancies, but loyally tries his best not to show it. When he cannot praise, he delivers himself of a silence so marked that a suspicious person could mistake it for suppressed criticism. However, he has plenty of opportunities to feel contented with the way things go—his book is full of them.

> King David of Scotland . . . under color of religion caused his followers to deal most barbarously with the English. They ripped open women, tossed children on the points of spears, butchered priests at the altars, and, cutting off the heads from the images on crucifixes, placed them on the bodies of the slain, while in exchange they fixed on the crucifixes the heads of their victims. Wherever the Scots came, there was the same scene of horror and cruelty: women shrieking, old men lamenting, amid the groans of the dying and the despair of the living.

But the English got the victory.

> Then the chief of the men of Lothian fell, pierced by an arrow, and all his followers were put to flight. For the Almighty was offended at them and their strength was rent like a cobweb.

Offended at them for what? For committing those fearful butcheries? No, for that was the common custom on both sides, and not open to criticism. Then was it for doing the butcheries "under cover of religion"? No, that was not it; religious feeling was often expressed in that fervent way all through those old centuries. The truth is, He was not offended at "them" at all; He was only offended at their king, who had been false to an oath. Then why did not He put the punishment upon the king instead of upon "them"? It is a difficult question. One can see by the Chronicle that the "judgments" fell rather customarily upon the wrong person, but Henry of Huntington does not explain why. Here is one that went true; the chronicler's satisfaction in it is not hidden:

In the month of August, Providence displayed its justice in a remarkable manner; for two of the nobles who had converted monasteries into fortifications, expelling the monks, their sin being the same, met with a similar punishment. Robert Marmion was one, Godfrey de Mandeville the other. Robert Marmion, issuing forth against the enemy, was slain under the walls of the monastery, being the only one who fell, though he was surrounded by his troops. Dying excommunicated, he became subject to death everlasting. In like manner Earl Godfrey was singled out among his followers, and shot with an arrow by a common foot-soldier. He made light of the wound, but he died of it in a few days, under excornmunication. See here the like judgment of God, memorable through all ages!

This exaltation jars upon me; not because of the death of the men, for they deserved that, but because it is death eternal, in white-hot fire and flame. It makes my flesh crawl. I have not known more than three men, or perhaps four, in my whole lifetime, whom I would rejoice to see writhing in those fires for even a year, let alone forever. I believe I would relent before the year was up, and get them out if I could. I think that in the long run, if a man's wife and babies, who had not harmed me, should come crying and pleading, I couldn't stand it; I know I should forgive him and let him go, even if he had violated a monastery. Henry of Huntington has been watching Godfrey and Marmion[11] for nearly seven hundred and fifty years, now, but I couldn't do it, I know I couldn't. I am soft and gentle in my nature, and I should have forgiven them seventy-and-seven times, long ago. And I think God has; but this is only an opinion, and not authoritative, like Henry of Huntington's interpretations. I could learn to interpret, but I have never tried; I get so little time.

All through his book Henry exhibits his familiarity with the intentions of God, and with the reasons for his intentions. Sometimes—very often, in fact—the act follows the intention after such a wide interval of time that one wonders how Henry could fit one act out of a hundred to one intention out of a hundred and get the thing right every time when there was such abundant choice among acts and intentions. Sometimes a man offends the Deity with a crime, and is punished for it thirty years later; meantime he has committed a million other crimes: no matter, Henry can pick out the one that brought the worms. Worms were generally used in those days for the slaying of particularly wicked people. This has gone out, now, but in old times it was a favorite. It always indicated a case of "wrath." For instance:

> . . . the just God avenging Robert Fitzhildebrand's perfidy, a worm grew in his vitals, which gradually gnawing its way through his intestines fattened on the abandoned man till, tortured with excruciating sufferings and venting himself in bitter moans, he was by a fitting punishment brought to his end.—(p. 400)

It was probably an alligator, but we cannot tell; we only know it was a particular breed, and only used to convey wrath. Some authorities think it was an ichthyosaurus, but there is much doubt.

However, one thing we do know; and that is that that worm had been due years and years. Robert F. had violated a monastery once; he had committed unprintable crimes since, and they had been permitted—under disapproval—but the ravishment of the monastery had not been forgotten nor forgiven, and the worm came at last.

Why were these reforms put off in this strange way? What was to be gained by it? Did Henry of Huntington really know his facts, or was he only guessing? Sometimes I am half persuaded that he is only a guesser, and not a good one. The divine wisdom must surely be of the better quality than he makes it out to be.

Five hundred years before Henry's time some forecasts of the Lord's purposes were furnished by a pope, who perceived, by certain perfectly trustworthy signs furnished by the Deity for the information of His familiars, that the end of the world was

> . . . about to come. But as this end of the world draws near, many things are at hand which have not before happened, as changes in the air, terrible signs in the heavens, tempests out of the common order of the seasons, wars, famines, pestilences, earthquakes in various places; all which win not happen in our days, but after our days all will come to pass.

Still, the end was so near that these signs were "sent before that we may be careful for our souls and be found prepared to meet the impending judgment."

That was thirteen hundred years ago. This is really no improvement on the work of the Roman augurs.

## NOTES

1. Jean-François Champollion (1790–1832), French historian and linguist, and the founder of scientific Egyptology. In 1821–22 he published several papers on the Rosetta Stone.

2. Twain appears to refer to Georg Friedrich Grotefend (1775–1853), German epigraphist. His work was chiefly in the area of Persian inscriptions. He did no work on the Rosetta Stone.

3. Fictitious. The word means "gentleman" in Serbo-Croatian.

4. Sir Henry Creswicke Rawlinson (1810–1895), British Assyriologist and diplomat. He did not work on the Rosetta Stone.

5. Twain refers to Napoleon's escape from exile on the island of Elba on February 26, 1815, but this event occurred well before the events described previously.

6. Dighton Rock is a geological formation near Taunton, Massachusetts, containing inscriptions that were once thought to have been made by Norse explorers but are now known to have been the work of Native Americans.

7. Twain refers to Alexander Thomson's translation of Suetonius' *Lives of the Twelve Caesars*, revised by Thomas Forester (London: H. G. Bohn, 1855). The citation is from *Augustus* 94.2.

8. *Augustus* 94.4.

9. *Augustus* 95.

10. Twain refers to the usurpation of the English throne by Stephen (1097–1154; r. 1135–54), as recounted in a Latin chronicle by Henry of Huntingdon (12th century). Throughout the essay Twain quotes from the edition of Huntingdon's *Chronicle* translated and edited by Thomas Forester (London: H. G. Bohn, 1853).

11. Godfrey of Bouillon (1060?–1100), leader of the first Crusade; the barons of Marmion, a British noble family.

# GOD
## (1905)

*H*e made all things. There is not in the universe a thing, great or small, which He did not make. He pronounced His work "good." The word covers the whole of it; it puts the seal of His approval upon each detail of it, it praises each detail of it. We also approve and praise—with our mouths. With our mouths we praise and approve the whole work. We do it loudly, we do it fervently—also judiciously. Judiciously. For we do not enter into particulars.

Daily we pour out freshets of disapproval, dispraise, censure, passionate resentment, upon a considerable portion of the work—but not with our mouths. No it is our acts that betray us, not our words. Our words are all compliments, and they deceive Him. Without a doubt they do. They make Him think we approve of all of His works.

That is the way we argue. For ages we have taught ourselves to believe that when we hide a disapproving fact, burying it under a mountain of complimentary lies, He is not aware of it, does not notice it, perceives only the compliments, and is deceived. But is it really so? Among ourselves we concede that acts speak louder than words, but we have persuaded ourselves that in His case it is different; we imagine that all He cares for is words—noise; that if we make the words pretty enough they will blind Him to the acts that give them the lie.

But seriously, does any one really believe that? Is it not a daring affront to the Supreme Intelligence to believe such a thing? Does any of us inordinately praise a mother's whole family to her face, indiscriminately, and in that same moment slap one of her children? Would not that act turn our inflamed eulogy into nonsense? Would the mother be deceived? Would she not be offended—and properly?

But see what we do in His case. We approve all His works, we praise all His works, with a fervent enthusiasm—of words; and in the same moment we kill a fly, which is as much one of His works as is any other, and has been included and complimented in our sweeping eulogy. We not only kill the fly, but we do it in a spirit of measureless disapproval—even a spirit of hatred, exasperation, vindictiveness; and we regard that creature with disgust and loathing—which is the essence of contempt—and yet we have just been praising it, approving it, glorifying it. We have been praising it to its Maker, and now our act insults its Maker. The praise was dishonest, the act is honest; the one was wordy hypocrisy, the other is compact candor.

We hunt the fly remorselessly; also the flea, the rat, the snake, the disease-germ and a thousand other creatures which He pronounced good, and was satisfied with, and which we loudly praise and approve—with our mouths—and then harry and chase and malignantly destroy, by wholesale.

Manifestly this is not well, not wise, not right. It breeds falsehood and sham. Would He be offended if we should change it and appear before Him with the truth in our mouths as well as in our acts? May we not, trustingly and without fear, change our words and say—

"O Source of Truth, we have lied, and we repent. Hear us confess that which we have felt from the beginning of time, but have weakly tried to conceal from Thee: humbly we praise and glorify many of Thy works, and are grateful for their presence in our earth, Thy footstool, but not all of them."

That would be sufficient. It would not be necessary to name the exceptions.

# CHRISTIAN CITIZENSHIP
## (1905)

*I*s there such a thing as Christian citizenship? No, but it could be created. The process would be quite simple, and not productive of hardship to any one. It will be conceded that every man's first duty is to God; it will also be conceded, and with strong emphasis, that a Christian's first duty is to God. It then follows, as a matter of course, that it is his duty to carry his Christian code of morals to the polls and vote them. Whenever he shall do that, he will not find himself voting for an unclean man, a dishonest man. Whenever a Christian votes, he votes against God or for Him, and he knows this quite well. God is an issue in every election; He is a candidate in the person of every clean nominee on every ticket; His purity and His approval are there, to be voted for or voted against, and no fealty to party can absolve His servant from his higher and more exacting fealty to Him; He takes precedence of party, duty to Him is above every claim of party.

If Christians should vote their duty to God at the polls, they would carry every election, and do it with ease. They would elect every clean candidate in the United States, and defeat every soiled one. Their prodigious power would be quickly realized and recognized, and afterward there would be no unclean candidates upon any ticket, and graft would cease. No church organization can be found in the country that would elect men of foul character to be its shepherd, its treasurer, and superintendent of its Sunday-school. It would be revolted at the idea; it would consider such an election an insult to God. Yet every Christian congregation in the country elects foul men to public office, while quite aware that this also is an open and deliberate insult to God, who can not approve and does not approve the placing of the liberties and the well-being of His children in the hands of infamous men. It is the Christian congregations that are responsible for the filling of our public offices with criminals, for the reason that they could prevent it if they chose to do it. They could prevent it without organizing a league, without framing a platform, without making any speeches or passing any resolutions—in a word, without concert of any kind. They could accomplish it by each individual resolving to vote for God at the polls—that is to say, vote for the candidate whom God would approve. Can a man imagine such a thing as God being a Republican or a Democrat, and voting for a criminal or a blackguard merely because party loyalty required it? Then can we imagine that a man can improve upon God's attitude in this matter, and by help of professional politicians invent a better policy? God has no politics but cleanliness and honesty, and it is good enough for men.

A man's second duty is to his family. There was a time when a clergyman's duty to his family required him to be his congregation's political slave, and vote his congregation's ticket in order to safeguard the food and shelter of his wife and children. But that time has gone by. We have the secret ballot now, and a clergyman can vote for God. He can also plead with his congregation to do the like.

Perhaps. We can not be sure. The congregation would probably inquire whom *he* was going to vote for; and if he stood upon his manhood and answered that they had no Christian right (which is the same as saying no moral right, and, of course, no legal right) to ask the question, it is conceivable—not to say certain—that they would dismiss him, and be much offended at his proposing to be a man as well as a clergyman.

Still, there are clergymen who are so situated as to be able to make the experiment. It would be worth while to try it. If the Christians of America could be persuaded to vote God and a clean ticket, it would bring about a moral revolution that would be incalculably beneficent. It would save the country—a country whose Christians have betrayed it and are destroying it.

The Christians of Connecticut sent Bulkeley to the Senate.[1] They sent to the Legislature the men who elected him. These two crimes they could have prevented; they did not do it, and upon them rest the shame and the responsibility. Only one clergyman remembered his Christian morals and his duty to God, and stood bravely by both. Mr. Smythe[2] is probably an outcast now, but such a man as that can endure ostracism; and such a man as that is likely to possess the treasure of a family that can endure it with him, and be proud to do it. I kiss the hem of his garment.

Four years ago Greater New York had two tickets in the field: one clean, the other dirty, with a single exception; an unspeakable ticket with that lonely exception.[3] One-half of the Christians voted for that foul ticket and against God and the Christian code of morals, putting loyalty to party above loyalty to God and honorable citizenship, and they came within a fraction of electing it; whereas if they had stood by their professed morals they would have buried it out of sight. Christianity was on trial then, it is on trial now. And nothing important is on trial except Christianity.

It was on trial in Philadelphia, and failed; in Pennsylvania, and failed; in Rhode Island, and failed; in Connecticut, and failed; in New York, and failed; in Delaware, and failed; in every town and county and State, and was recreant to its trust; it has effusively busied itself with the small matters of charity and benevolence, and has looked on, indifferent while its country was sinking lower and lower in repute and drifting further and further toward moral destruction. It is the one force that can save, and it sits with folded hands. In Greater New York it will presently have an opportunity to elect or defeat some straight, clean, honest men, of the sterling Jerome stamp,[4] and some of the Tammany kind. The Christian vote—and the Christian vote alone—will decide the contest. It, and it alone, is master of the situation, and lord of the result.

## NOTES

1. Morgan Bulkeley (1837–1922), president of the Aetna Life Insurance Company, Republican governor of Connecticut (1888–92), and US senator from Connecticut (1905–11). Bulkeley's governorship was marred by a suspicion of illegitimacy (he received fewer votes than his opponent, but the Republican-controlled legislature nonetheless voted to seat him) and by difficulty in working with a divided legislature.

2. Newman Smyth (not Smythe) (1843–1925), pastor of the First Church of Christ (Congregational), New Haven (1882–1908).

3. Twain refers to the successful mayoral campaign of Seth Low (1850–1916), a reform candidate who, in the election of 1901, narrowly defeated Edward Morse Shepard, a candidate chosen by the corrupt Tammany incumbent, Robert Van Wyck.

4. William Travers Jerome (1859–1934), New York City district attorney (1901–1909) who won reelection in 1905. Twain actively worked on his campaign. In the mayoral election of that year, however, the Tammany candidate, George B. McClellan, who had defeated Seth Low in 1903, was reelected.

# THE TEN COMMANDMENTS
## (1905 or 1906)

*T*he Ten Commandments were made for man alone. We should think it strange if they had been made for *all* the animals.

We should say "Thou shalt not kill" is too general, too sweeping. It includes the field mouse and the butterfly. They *can't* kill. And it includes the tiger, which can't *help* it.

It is a case of Temperament and Circumstance again. You can arrange no circumstances that can move the field mouse and the butterfly to kill; their temperaments will keep them unaffected by temptations to kill, they can avoid that crime without an effort. But it isn't so with the tiger. Throw a lamb in his way when he is hungry, and his temperament will compel him to kill it.

Butterflies and field mice are common among men; they can't kill, their temperaments make it impossible. There are tigers among men, also. Their temperaments move them to violence, and when Circumstance furnishes the opportunity and the powerful motive, they kill. They can't help it.

No penal law can deal out *justice*; it must deal out injustice in every instance. Penal laws have a high value, in that they protect—in a considerable measure—the multitude of the gentle-natured from the violent minority.

For a penal law is a Circumstance. It is a warning which intrudes and stays a would-be murderer's hand—sometimes. Not always, but in many and many a case. It can't stop the *real* man-tiger; nothing can do that. Slade had 26 deliberate murders on his soul when he finally went to his death on the scaffold.[1] He would kill a man for a trifle; or for nothing. He loved to kill. It was his temperament. He did not make his temperament, God gave it him at his birth. Gave it him and said Thou shalt not kill. It was like saying Thou shalt not eat. Both appetites were given him at birth. He could be obedient and starve both up to a certain point, but that was as far as he could go. Another man could go further; but not Slade.

Holmes, the Chicago monster,[2] inveigled some dozens of men and women into his obscure quarters and privately butchered them. Holmes's inborn nature was such that whenever he had what seemed a reasonably safe opportunity to kill a stranger he couldn't successfully resist the temptation to do it.

Justice was finally meted out to Slade and to Holmes. That is what the newspapers said. It is a common phrase, and a very old one. But it probably isn't true. When a man is hanged for slaying one man that phrase comes into service and we learn that justice was meted out to the slayer. But Holmes slew sixty. There seems to be a discrepancy in this distribution of justice. If Holmes got justice, the other man got 59 times more than justice.

But the phrase is wrong, anyway. The *word* is the wrong word. Criminal courts do not dispense "justice"—they *can't*; they only dispense protections to the community. It is all they can do.

## NOTES

1. Joseph Alfred ("Jack") Slade (1829?–1864), son of a US congressman who was hired by various companies in the West to protect stagecoaches, freight, and the like. Twain had met him at the Rocky Ridge station in Wyoming.

2. H. H. Holmes (pseudonym of Herman Webster Mudgett, 1860–1896), who may have committed hundreds of murders during the Chicago World's Fair of 1893. He confessed to twenty-seven murders. He was hanged in Philadelphia on May 7, 1896.

# Reflections on Religion
## (1906)

## I

*Tuesday, June 19, 1906*

*O*ur Bible reveals to us the character of our God with minute and remorseless exactness. The portrait is substantially that of a man—if one can imagine a man charged and overcharged with evil impulses far beyond the human limit; a personage whom no one, perhaps, would desire to associate with now that Nero and Caligula are dead. In the Old Testament His acts expose His vindictive, unjust, ungenerous, pitiless and vengeful nature constantly. He is always punishing—punishing trifling misdeeds with thousandfold severity; punishing innocent children for the misdeeds of their parents; punishing unoffending populations for the misdeeds of their rulers; even descending to wreak bloody vengeance upon harmless calves and lambs and sheep and bullocks as punishment for inconsequential trespasses committed by their proprietors. It is perhaps the most damnatory biography that exists in print anywhere. It makes Nero an angel of light and leading by contrast.

It begins with an inexcusable treachery, and that is the keynote of the entire biography. That beginning must have been invented in a pirate's nursery, it is so malign and so childish. To Adam is forbidden the fruit of a certain tree—and he is gravely informed that if he disobeys he shall die. How could that be expected to impress Adam? Adam was merely a man in stature; in knowledge and experience he was in no way the superior of a baby of two years of age; he could have no idea of what the word death meant. He had never seen a dead thing; he had never heard of a dead thing before. The word meant nothing to him. If the Adam child had been warned that if he ate of the apples he would be transformed into a meridian of longitude, that threat would have been the equivalent of the other, since neither of them could mean anything to him.

The watery intellect that invented the memorable threat could be depended on to supplement it with other banalities and low grade notions of justice and fairness, and that is what happened. It was decreed that all of Adam's descendants, to the latest day, should be punished for the baby's trespass against a law of his nursery fulminated against him before he was out of his diapers. For thousands and thousands of years his posterity, individual by individual, has been unceasingly hunted and harried with afflictions in punishment of the juvenile misdemeanor which is grandiloquently called Adam's Sin. And during all that vast lapse of time there has been no lack of rabbins and popes and bishops and priests and parsons and lay slaves eager to applaud this infamy, maintain the unassailable justice and righteousness of it, and praise its Author in terms of flattery so gross and extravagant that none but a God could listen to it and not hide His face in disgust and embarrassment. Hardened to flattery as our Oriental potentates are through long experience, not even they would be able to endure the rank quality of it which our God endures with complacency and satisfaction from our pulpits every Sunday.

We brazenly call our God the source of mercy, while we are aware all the time that there is not an authentic instance in history of His ever having exercised that virtue. We call Him the source of morals, while we know by His history and by His daily conduct as perceived with our own senses that He is totally destitute of anything resembling morals. We call Him Father, and not in derision, although we would detest and denounce any earthly father who should inflict upon his child a thousandth part of the pains and miseries and cruelties which our God deals out to His children every day, and has dealt out to them daily during all the centuries since the crime of creating Adam was committed.

We deal in a curious and laughable confusion of notions concerning God. We divide Him in two, bring half of Him down to an obscure and infinitesimal corner of the world to confer salvation upon a little colony of Jews—and only Jews, no one else—and leave the other half of Him throned in Heaven and looking down and eagerly and anxiously watching for results. We reverently study the history of the earthly half and deduce from it the conviction that the earthly half has reformed, is equipped with morals and virtues, and in no way resembles the abandoned, malignant half that abides upon the throne. We conceive that the earthly half is just, merciful, charitable, benevolent, forgiving and full of sympathy for the sufferings of mankind and anxious to remove them. Apparently we deduce this character not by examining facts but by diligently declining to search them, measure them and weigh them. The earthly half requires us to be merciful and sets us an example by inventing a lake of fire and brimstone in which all of us who fail to recognize and worship Him as God are to be burned through all eternity. And not only we, who are offered these terms, are to be thus burned if we neglect them, but also the earlier billions of human beings are to suffer this awful fate, although they all lived and died without ever having heard of Him or the terms at all. This exhibition of mercifulness may be called gorgeous. We have nothing approaching it among human savages, nor among the wild beasts of the jungle. We are required to forgive our brother seventy times seven times and be satisfied and content if on our death-bed, after a pious life, our soul escape from our body before the hurrying priest can get to us and furnish it a pass with his mumblings and candles and incantations. This example of the forgiving spirit may also be pronounced gorgeous.

We are told that the two halves of our God are only seemingly disconnected by their separation; that in very fact the two halves remain one, and equally powerful, notwithstanding the separation. This being the case, the earthly half—who mourns over the sufferings of mankind and would like to remove them, and is quite competent to remove them at any moment He may choose—satisfies Himself with restoring sight to a blind person here and there instead of restoring it to all the blind; cures a cripple here and there instead of curing all the cripples; furnishes to five thousand famishing persons a meal and lets the rest of the millions that are hungry remain hungry—and all the time He admonishes inefficient man to cure these ills which God Himself inflicted upon him, and which He could extinguish with a word if He chose to do it, and thus do a plain duty which He had neglected from the beginning and always will neglect while time shall last. He raised several dead persons to life. He manifestly regarded this as a kindness. If it was a kindness it was not just to confine it to half-a-dozen persons. He should have raised the rest of the dead. I would not do it myself, for I think the dead are the only human beings who are really well off—but I merely mention it in passing as one of those curious incongruities with which our Bible history is heavily over-charged.

Whereas the God of the Old Testament is a fearful and repulsive character He is at least consistent. He is frank and outspoken. He makes no pretense to the possession of a moral or a virtue of any kind—except with His mouth. No such thing is anywhere discoverable in His conduct. I think He comes infinitely nearer to being respectworthy than does His reformed self as guilelessly exposed in the New Testament. Nothing in all history—nor even His massed history combined—remotely approaches in atrocity the invention of Hell.

His heavenly self, His Old Testament self, is sweetness and gentleness and respectability, compared with His reformed earthly self. In Heaven he claims not a single merit and hasn't one—outside of those claimed by His mouth—whereas in the earth He claims every merit in the entire catalogue of merits, yet practised them only now and then, penuriously, and finished by conferring Hell upon us, which abolished all His fictitious merits in a body.

# II

*Wednesday, June 20, 1906*

There are one or two curious defects about Bibles. An almost pathetic poverty of invention characterizes them all. That is one striking defect. Another is that each pretends to originality without possessing any. Each borrows from the others and gives no credit, which is a distinctly immoral act. Each in turn confiscates decayed old stage-properties from the others and with naive confidence puts them forth as fresh new inspirations from on high. We borrow the Golden Rule from Confucius after it has seen service for centuries and copyright it without a blush.[1] When we want a Deluge we go away back to hoary Babylon and borrow it, and are as proud of it and as satisfied with it as if it had been worth the trouble. We still revere it and admire it today and claim that it came to us direct from the mouth of the Deity; whereas we know that Noah's flood never happened, and couldn't have happened. The flood is a favorite with Bible makers. If there is a Bible—or even a tribe of savages—that lacks a General Deluge it is only because the religious scheme that lacks it hadn't any handy source to borrow it from.

Another prime favorite with the authors of sacred literature and founders of religions is the Immaculate Conception. It had been worn threadbare before we adopted it as a fresh new idea—and we admire it as much now as did the original conceiver of it when his mind was delivered of it a million years ago. The Hindus prized it ages ago when they acquired Krishna by the Immaculate process. Process. The Buddhists were happy when they acquired Gautama by the same process twenty-five hundred years ago. The Greeks of the same period had great joy in it when their Supreme Being and his cabinet used to come down and people Greece with mongrels half human and half divine. The Romans borrowed the idea from Greece and found great happiness in Jupiter's Immaculate Conception products. We got it direct from Heaven, by way of Rome. We are still charmed with it. And only a fortnight ago, when an Episcopal clergyman in Rochester was summoned before the governing body of his church to answer the charge of intimating that he did not believe that the Savior was miraculously conceived, the Rev. Dr. Briggs, who is perhaps the most daringly broad-minded religious person now occupying an American pulpit, took up the cudgels in favor of the Immaculate Conception in an article in the *North American Review*, and from the tone of that article it seemed apparent that he believed he had settled that vexed question once and for all.[2] His idea was that there could be no doubt about it, for the reason that the Virgin Mary knew it was authentic because the Angel of the Annunciation told her so. Also, it must have been so, for the additional reason that Jude—a later son of Mary, the Virgin, and born in wedlock—was still living and associating with the adherents of the early church many years after the event, and that he said quite decidedly that it was a case of Immaculate Conception; therefore it must be true, for Jude was right there in the family and in a position to know.

If there is anything more amusing than the Immaculate Conception doctrine it is the quaint reasonings whereby ostensibly intelligent human beings persuade themselves that the impossible fact is proven.

If Dr. Briggs were asked to believe in the Immaculate Conception as exercised in the cases of Krishna, Osiris, Buddha and the rest of the tribe he would decline with thanks and probably be offended. If pushed, he would probably say that it would be childish to believe in those cases, for the reason that they were supported by none but human testimony and that it would be impossible to prove such a thing by human testimony, because if the entire human race were present at a case of Immaculate Conception they wouldn't be able to tell when it happened, nor whether it happened at all—and yet this bright man with the temporarily muddy mind is quite able to believe an impossibility whose authenticity rests entirely upon human testimony—the testimony of but one human being, the Virgin herself, a witness not disinterested, but powerfully interested; a witness incapable of knowing the fact as a fact, but getting all that she supposed she knew about it at second hand—at second hand from an entire stranger, an alleged angel, who could have been an angel, perhaps, but also could have been a tax collector. It is not likely that she had ever seen an angel before or knew their trade-marks. He was a stranger. He brought no credentials. His evidence was worth nothing at all to anybody else in the community. It is worth nothing today to any but minds which are like Dr. Briggs's—which have lost their clarity through mulling over absurdities in the pious wish to dig something sane and rational out of them. The Immaculate Conception rests wholly upon the testimony of a single witness—a witness whose testimony is without value—a witness whose very existence has nothing to rest upon but the assertion of the young peasant wife whose husband needed to be pacified. Mary's testimony satisfied him but that is because he lived in Nazareth instead of New York. There isn't any carpenter in New York that would take the testimony at par. If the Immaculate Conception could be repeated in New York today there isn't a man, woman or child of those four millions who would believe in it—except perhaps some addled Christian Scientists. A person who can believe in Mother Eddy[3] wouldn't strain at an Immaculate Conception, or six of them in a bunch. The Immaculate Conception could not be repeated successfully in New York in our day. It would produce laughter, not reverence and adoration.

To a person who doesn't believe in it, it seems a most puerile invention. It could occur to nobody but a god that it was a large and ingenious arrangement and had dignity in it. It could occur to nobody but a god that a divine Son procured through promiscuous relations with a peasant family in a village could improve the purity of the product, yet that is the very idea. The product acquires purity—purity absolute—purity from all stain or blemish—through a gross violation of both human and divine law, as set forth in the constitution and by-laws of the Bible. Thus the Christian religion, which requires everybody to be moral and to obey the laws, has its very beginning in immorality and in disobedience to law. You couldn't purify a tomcat by the Immaculate Conception process.

Apparently as a pious stage-property it is still useful, still workable, although it is so bent with age and so nearly exhausted by overwork. It is another case of begats. What's-his-name begat Krishna, Krishna begat Buddha, Buddha begat Osiris, Osiris begat the Babylonian deities, they begat God, He begat Jesus, Jesus begat Mrs. Eddy. If she is going to continue the line and do her proper share of the begatting, she must get at it, for she is already an antiquity.

There is one notable thing about our Christianity: bad, bloody, merciless, money-grabbing and predatory as it is—in our country particularly, and in all other Christian countries in a somewhat modified degree—it is still a hundred times better than the Christianity of the Bible, with its prodigious crime—the invention of Hell. Measured by our Christianity of today, bad as it is, hypocritical as it is, empty and hollow as it is, neither the Deity nor His Son is a Christian, nor qualified for that moderately high place. Ours is a terrible religion. The fleets of the world could swim in spacious comfort in the innocent blood it has spilt.

# III

*Friday, June 22, 1906*

For two years now Christianity has been repeating in Russia the sort of industries in the way of massacre and mutilation with which it has been successfully persuading Christendom in every century for nineteen hundred years that it is the only right and true religion—the one and only religion of peace and love. For two years now the ultra-Christian Government of Russia had been officially ordering and conducting massacres of its Jewish subjects. These massacres have been so frequent that we have become almost indifferent to them. The accounts of them hardly affect us more than do accounts of corners in a railroad stock in which we have no money invested. We have become so used to their described horrors that we hardly shudder now when we read of them.

Here are some of the particulars of one of the latest efforts of these humble Twentieth Century disciples to persuade the unbeliever to come into the fold of the meek and gentle Savior.[4]

Horrible details have been sent out by the correspondent of the Bourse Gazette, who arrived in Bialystok in company with Deputy Schepkin on Saturday, and who managed to send his story by a messenger Sunday afternoon. The correspondent, who accompanied Schepkin directly to the hospital escorted by a Corporal's guard, says he was utterly unnerved by the sights he witnessed there.

"Merely saying that the bodies were mutilated," the correspondent writes, "fails to describe the awful facts. The faces of the dead have lost all human resemblance. The body of Teacher Apstein lay on the grass with the hands tied. In the face and eyes had been hammered three-inch nails. Rioters entered his home, killing him thus, and then murdered the rest of his family of seven. When the body arrived at the hospital it was also marked with bayonet thrusts.

"Beside the body of Apstein lay that of a child of 10 years, whose leg had been chopped off with an axe. Here also were the dead from the Schlachter home, where, according to witnesses, soldiers came and plundered the house and killed the wife, son, and a neighbor's daughter and seriously wounded Schlachter and his two daughters.

"I am told that soldiers entered the apartments of the Lapidus brothers, which were crowded with people who had fled from the streets for safety, and ordered the Christians to separate themselves from the Jews. A Christian student named Dikar protested and was killed on the spot. Then all of the Jews were shot."

From the wounded in the hospital the correspondent heard many pitiable stories, all of the same general tenor. Here is the account of a badly wounded merchant named Nevyazhiky:

"I live in the suburbs. Learning of the pogrom, I tried to reach the town through the fields, but was intercepted by roughs. My brother was killed, my arm and leg were broken, my skull was fractured, and I was stabbed twice in the side. I fainted from loss of blood, and revived to find a soldier standing over me, who asked: 'What, are you still alive! Shall I bayonet you?' I begged him to spare my life. The roughs again came, but spared me, saying: 'He will die; let him suffer longer.'"

The correspondent, who adopts the bitterest tone toward the government, holds that the pogrom undoubtedly was provoked, and attributes the responsibility to Police Lieutenant Sheremetieff. He declares that not only the soldiers, but their officers, participated, and that he himself was a witness as late as Saturday to the shooting down of a Jewish girl from the window of a hotel by Lieut. Miller of the Vladimir Regiment. The Governor of the Province of Grodno, who happened to be passing at the moment, ordered an investigation.

The pulpit and the optimist are always talking about the human race's steady march toward ultimate perfection. As usual, they leave out the statistics. It is the pulpit's way—the optimist's way.

Is there any discoverable advance toward moderation between the massacre of the Albigenses[5] and these massacres of Russian Jews? There is one difference. In elaborate cruelty and brutality the modern massacre exceeds the ancient one. Is any advance discoverable between Batholomew's Day[6] and these Jewish massacres? Yes. The same difference again appears: the modern Russian Christian and his Czar have advanced to an extravagance of bloody and bestial atrocity undreamed of by their crude brethren of three hundred and thirty-five years ago.

The Gospel of Peace is always making a good deal of noise with its mouth; always rejoicing in the progress it is making toward final perfection, and always diligently neglecting to furnish the statistics. George the Third reigned sixty years, the longest reign in English history up to his time. When his revered successor, Victoria, turned the sixty-year corner—thus scoring a new long-reign record—the event was celebrated with great pomp and circumstance and public rejoicing in England and her colonies. Among the statistics fetched out for general admiration were these: that for each year of the sixty of her reign Victoria's Christian soldiers had fought in a separate and distinct war. Meantime the possessions of England had swollen to such a degree by depredations committed upon helpless and godless pagans that there were not figures enough in Great Britain to set down the stolen acreage and they had to import a lot from other countries.

There are no peaceful nations now except those unhappy ones whose borders have not been invaded by the Gospel of Peace. All Christendom is a soldier-camp. During all the past generation the Christian poor have been taxed almost to starvation-point to support the giant armaments which the Christian Governments have built up, each to protect itself from the rest of the brotherhood and, incidentally, to snatch any patch of real estate left exposed by its savage owner. King Leopold II of Belgium[7]—probably the most intensely Christian monarch, except Alexander the Sixth,[8] that has escaped Hell thus far—has stolen an entire kingdom in Africa, and in the fourteen years of Christian endeavor there has reduced the population of thirty millions to fifteen by murder, mutilation, overwork, robbery, rapine—confiscating the helpless native's very labor and giving him nothing in return but salvation and a home in Heaven, furnished at the last moment by the Christian priest.

Within this last generation each Christian power has turned the bulk of its attention to finding out newer and still newer and more and more effective ways of killing Christians—and, incidentally, a pagan now and then—and the surest way to get rich quickly in Christ's earthly kingdom is to invent a gun that can kill more Christians at one shot than any other existing gun.

Also, during the same generation each Christian Government has played with its neighbors a continuous poker game in the naval line. In this game France puts up a battleship; England sees that battleship and goes it one battleship better; Russia comes in and raises it a battleship or two—*did*, before the untaught stranger entered the game and reduced her stately pile of chips to a damaged ferryboat and a cruiser that can't cruise. We are in it ourselves now. This game goes on and on and on. There is never a new shuffle; never a new deal. No player ever calls another's hand. It is merely an unending game of put up and put up and put up; and by the law of probabilities a day is coming when no Christians will be left on the land, except the women. The men will all be at sea, manning the fleets.

This singular game, which is so costly and so ruinous and so silly, is called statesmanship—which is different from assmanship on account of the spelling. Anybody but a statesman could invent some way to reduce these vast armaments to rational and sensible and safe police proportions, with the result that thenceforth all Christians could sleep in their beds unafraid, and even the Savior could come down and walk on the seas, foreigner as He is, without dread of being chased by Christian battleships.

Has the Bible done something still worse than drench the planet with innocent blood? To my mind it has—but this is only an opinion, and it may be a mistaken one. There has never been a Protestant boy or a Protestant girl whose mind the Bible has not soiled. No Protestant child ever comes clean from association with the Bible. This association cannot be prevented. Sometimes the parents try to prevent it by not allowing the children to have access to the Bible's awful obscenities, but this only whets the child's desire to taste that forbidden fruit, and it does taste it—seeks it out secretly and devours it with a strong and grateful appetite. The Bible does its baleful work in the propagation of vice among children, and vicious and unclean ideas, daily and constantly, in every Protestant family in Christendom. It does more of this deadly work than all the other unclean books in Christendom put together; and not only more, but a thousandfold more. It is easy to protect the young from those other books, and they are protected from them. But they have no protection against the deadly Bible.

Is it doubted that the young people hunt out the forbidden passages privately and study them with pleasure? If my reader were here present— let him be of either sex or any age, between ten and ninety—I would make him answer this question himself—and he could answer it in only one way. He would be obliged to say that by his own knowledge and experience of the days of his early youth he knows positively that the Bible defiles all Protestant children, without a single exception.

Do I think the Christian religion is here to stay? Why should I think so? There had been a thousand religions before it was born. They are all dead. There had been millions of gods before ours was invented. Swarms of them are dead and forgotten long ago. Ours is by long odds the worst God that the ingenuity of man has begotten from his insane imagina- tion—and shall He and His Christianity be immortal against the great array of probabilities furnished by the theological history of the past? No. I think that Christianity and its God must follow the rule. They must pass on in their turn and make room for another God and a stupider religion. Or perhaps a better than this? No. That is not likely. History shows that in the matter of religions we progress backward and not the other way. No matter, there will be a new God and a new religion. They will be intro- duced to popularity and accepted with the only arguments that have ever persuaded any people in this earth to adopt Christianity, or any other reli- gion that they were not born to: the Bible, the sword, the torch and the axe—the only missionaries that have ever scored a single victory since gods and religions began in the world. After the new God and the new religion have become established in the usual proportions—one-fifth of the world's population ostensible adherents, the four-fifths pagan missionary field, with the missionary scratching its continental back complacently and inef- ficiently—will the new converts believe in them? Certainly they will. They have always believed in the million gods and religions that have been stuffed down their midriffs. There isn't anything so grotesque or so incred- ible that the average human being can't believe it. At this very day there are thousands upon thousands of Americans of average intelligence who fully believe in *Science and Health*, although they can't understand a line of it, and who also worship the sordid and ignorant old purloiner of that gospel—Mrs. Mary Baker G. Eddy, whom they do absolutely believe to be a member by adoption of the Holy Family and on the way to push the Savior to third place and assume occupancy of His present place and continue that occupancy during the rest of eternity.

# IV

## Saturday, June 23, 1906

Let us now consider the real God, the genuine God, the great God, the sublime and supreme God, the authentic Creator of the real universe, whose remotenesses are visited by comets only—comets unto which incredibly distant Neptune is merely an outpost, a Sandy Hook to homeward-bound spectres of the deeps of space that have not glimpsed it before for generations—a universe not made with hands and suited to an astronomical nursery, but spread abroad through the illimitable reaches of space by the flat of the real God just mentioned; that God of unthinkable grandeur and majesty, by comparison with whom all the other gods whose myriads infest the feeble imaginations of men are as a swarm of gnats scattered and lost in the infinitudes of the empty sky.

When we think of such a God as this we cannot associate with Him anything trivial, anything lacking dignity, anything lacking grandeur. We cannot conceive of His passing by Sirius to choose our potato for a footstool. We cannot conceive of His interesting Himself in the affairs of the microscopic human race and enjoying its Sunday flatteries and experiencing pangs of jealousy when the flatteries grow lax or fail, any more than we can conceive of the Emperor of China being interested in a bottle of microbes and pathetically anxious to stand well with them and harvest their impertinent compliments. If we could conceive of the Emperor of China taking an intemperate interest in his bottle of microbes we should have to draw the line there; we could not by any stretch of imagination conceive of his selecting from these innumerable millions a quarter of a thimbleful of Jew microbes—the least attractive of the whole swarm—and making pets of them and nominating them as his chosen germs and carrying his infatuation for them so far as to resolve to keep and coddle them alone and damn all the rest.

When we examine the myriad wonders and glories and charms and perfections of this infinite universe (as we know the universe now), and perceive that there is not a detail of it—from the blade of grass to the giant trees of California, nor from the obscure mountain rivulet to the measureless ocean; nor from the ebb and flow of the tides to the stately motions of the planets—that is not the slave of a system of exact and inflexible law, we seem to know—not suppose nor conjecture, but *know*—that the God that brought this stupendous fabric into being with a flash of thought and framed its laws with another flash of thought is endowed with limitless power. We seem to know that whatever thing He wishes to do, He can do that thing without anybody's assistance. We also seem to know that when He flashed the universe into being He foresaw everything that would happen in it from that moment until the end of time.

Do we also know that He is a moral being, according to our standard of morals? No. If we know anything at all about it we know that He is destitute of morals—at least of the human pattern. Do we know that He is just, charitable, kindly, gentle, merciful, compassionate? No. There is no evidence that He is any of these things—whereas each and every day as it passes furnishes us a thousand volumes of evidence, and indeed proof, that He possesses none of these qualities.

When we pray, when we beg, when we implore, does He listen? Does He answer? There is not a single authentic instance of it in human history. Does He silently refuse to listen—refuse to answer? There is nothing resembling proof that He has ever done anything else. From the beginning of time priests, who have imagined themselves to be His appointed and salaried servants, have gathered together their full numerical strength and simultaneously prayed for rain and never once got it when it was not due according to the eternal laws of Nature. Whenever they got it, if they had had a competent Weather Bureau they could have saved themselves the trouble of praying for that rain, because the Bureau could have told them it was coming anyhow within twenty-four hours, whether they prayed or saved their sacred wind.

From the beginning of time whenever a king has lain dangerously ill the priesthood and some part of the nation have prayed in unison that the king be spared to his grieving and anxious people (in case they were grieving and anxious, which was not usually the rule) and in no instance was their prayer ever answered. When Mr. Garfield lay near to death, the physicians and surgeons knew that nothing could save him, yet at an appointed signal all the pulpits in the United States broke forth with one simultaneous and supplicating appeal for the President's restoration to health. They did this with the same old innocent confidence with which the primeval savage had prayed to his imaginary devils to spare his perishing chief—for that day will never come when facts and experience can teach a pulpit anything useful. Of course the President died just the same.[9]

Great Britain has a population of forty-one millions. She has eighty thousand pulpits. The Boer population was a hundred and fifty thousand, with a battery of two hundred and ten pulpits. In the beginning of the Boer war, at a signal from the Primate of all England the eighty thousand English pulpits thundered forth a titanic simultaneous supplication to their God to give the embattled English in South Africa the victory. The little Boer battery of two hundred and ten guns replied with a simultaneous supplication to the same God to give the Boers the victory. If the eighty thousand English clergy had left their prayers unshed and gone to the field they would have got it—whereas the victory went the other way and the English forces suffered defeat after defeat at the hands of the Boers. The English pulpit kept discreetly quiet about the result of its effort, but the indiscreet Boer pulpit proclaimed with a loud and exultant voice that it was *its* prayers that had conferred the victory upon the Boers.

The British Government had more confidence in soldiers than in prayer—therefore instead of doubling and trebling the numerical strength of the clergy it doubled and trebled the strength of its forces in the field. Then the thing happened that always happens—the English whipped the fight, a rather plain indication that the Lord had not listened to either side and was as indifferent as to who should win as He had always been, from the day that He was evolved down to the present time—there being no instance on record where He has shown any interest at all in any human squabble, nor whether the good cause won out or lost.

Has this experience taught the pulpit anything? It has not. When the Boer prayers achieved victory—as the Boers believed—the Boers were confirmed once more in their trust in the power of prayer. When a crushing finality of defeat overwhelmed them later in the face of their confident supplications, their attitude was not altered, nor their confidence in the righteousness and intelligence of God impaired.

Often we see a mother who has been despoiled little by little of everything she held dear in life but a sole remaining dying child; we have seen her, I say, kneeling by its bed and pouring out from a breaking heart beseechings to God for mercy that would get glad and instant answer from any man who had the power to save that child—yet no such prayer has ever moved a God to pity. Has that mother been convinced? Sometimes—but only for a little while. She was merely a human being and like the rest—ready to pray again in the next emergency; ready to believe again that she would be heard.

We know that the real God, the Supreme God, the actual Maker of the universe, made everything that is in it. We know that He made all the creatures, from the microbe and the brontosaur down to man and the monkey, and that He knew what would happen to each and every one of them from the beginning of time to the end of it. In the case of each creature, big or little, He made it an unchanging law that that creature should suffer wanton and unnecessary pains and miseries every day of its life—that by that law these pains and miseries could not be avoided by any diplomacy exercisable by the creature; that its way, from birth to death, should be beset by traps, pitfalls and gins, ingeniously planned and ingeniously concealed; and that by another law every transgression of a law of Nature, either ignorantly or wittingly committed, should in every instance be visited by a punishment ten-thousandfold out of proportion of the transgression. We stand astonished at the all-comprehensive malice which could patiently descend to the contriving of elaborate tortures for the meanest and pitifulest of the countless kinds of creatures that were to inhabit the earth. The spider was so contrived that she would not eat grass but must catch flies and such things and inflict a slow and horrible death upon them, unaware that her turn would come next. The wasp was so contrived that he also would decline grass and stab the spider, not conferring upon her a swift and merciful death, but merely half-paralyzing her, then ramming her down into the wasp den, there to live and suffer for days while the wasp babies should chew her legs off at their leisure. In turn, there was a murderer provided for the wasp, and another murderer for the wasp's murderer, and so on throughout the whole scheme of living creatures in the earth. There isn't one of them that was not designed and appointed to inflict misery and murder on some fellow creature and suffer the same in turn from some other murderous fellow creature. In flying into the web the fly is merely guilty of an indiscretion—not a breach of any law—yet the fly's punishment is ten-thousandfold out of proportion to that little indiscretion.

The ten-thousandfold law of punishment is rigorously enforced against every creature, man included. The debt, whether made innocently or guiltily, is promptly collected by Nature—and in this world, without waiting for the ten-billionfold additional penalty appointed—in the case of man—for collection in the next.

This system of atrocious punishments for somethings and nothings begins upon the helpless baby on its first day in the world and never ceases until its last one. Is there a father who would persecute his baby with unearned colics and the unearned miseries of teething, and follow these with mumps, measles, scarlet-fever and the hundred other persecutions appointed for the unoffending creature? And then follow these, from youth to the grave, with a multitude of ten-thousandfold punishments for laws broken either by intention or indiscretion? With a fine sarcasm we ennoble God with the title of Father—yet we know quite well that we should hang His style of father wherever we might catch him.

The pulpit's explanation of and apology for these crimes is pathetically destitute of ingenuity. It says that they are committed for the benefit of the sufferer. They are to discipline him, purify him, elevate him, train him for the society of the Deity and the angels—send him up sanctified with cancers, tumors, smallpox and the rest of the educational plant; whereas the pulpit knows that it is stultifying itself, if it knows anything at all. It knows that if this kind of discipline is wise and salutary, we are insane not to adopt it ourselves and apply it to our children.

Does the pulpit really believe that we can improve a purifying and elevating breed of culture invented by the Almighty? It seems to me that if the pulpit honestly believed what it is preaching in this regard it would recommend every father to imitate the Almighty's methods.

When the pulpit has succeeded in persuading its congregation that this system has been really wisely and mercifully contrived by the Almighty to discipline and purify and elevate His children whom He so loves, the pulpit judiciously closes its mouth. It doesn't venture further and explain why these same crimes and cruelties are inflicted upon the higher animals—the alligators, the tigers and the rest. It even proclaims that the beasts perish—meaning that their sorrowful life begins and ends here; that they go no further; that there is no Heaven for them; that neither God nor the angels nor the redeemed desire their society on the other side. It puts the pulpit in a comical situation, because in spite of all its ingenuities of explanation and apology it convicts its God of being a wanton and pitiless tyrant in the case of the unoffending beasts. At any rate, and beyond cavil or argument, by its silence it condemns Him irrevocably as a malignant master, after having persuaded the congregation that He is constructed entirely out of compassion, righteousness and all-pervading love. The pulpit doesn't know how to reconcile these grotesque contradictions and it doesn't try.

In His destitution of one and all of the qualities which could grace a God and invite respect for Him and reverence and worship, the real God, the genuine God, the Maker of the mighty universe is just like all the other gods in the list. He proves every day that He takes no interest in man, nor in the other animals, further than to torture them, slay them and get out of this pastime such entertainment as it may afford—and do what He can not to get weary of the eternal and changeless monotony of it.

# V

*Monday, June 25, 1906*

It is to these celestial bandits that the naive and confiding and illogical human rabbit looks for a Heaven of eternal bliss, which is to be his reward for patiently enduring the want and sufferings inflicted upon him here below—unearned sufferings covering terms of two or three years in some cases; five or ten years in others; thirty, forty or fifty in others; sixty, seventy, eighty in others. As usual, where the Deity is Judge the rewards are vastly out of proportion to the sufferings—and there is no system about the matter anyhow. You do not get any more Heaven for suffering eighty years than you get if you die of the measles at three.

There is no evidence that there is to be a Heaven hereafter. If we should find, somewhere, an ancient book in which a dozen unknown men professed to tell all about a blooming and beautiful tropical Paradise secreted in an inaccessible valley in the center of the eternal icebergs which constitute the Antarctic continent—not claiming that they had seen it themselves, but had acquired an intimate knowledge of it through a revelation from God—no Geographical Society in the earth would take any stock in that book; yet that book would be quite as authentic, quite as trustworthy, quite as valuable evidence as is the Bible. The Bible is just like it. Its Heaven exists solely upon hearsay evidence—evidence furnished by unknown persons; persons who did not prove that they had ever been there.

If Christ had really been God He could have proved it, since nothing is impossible with God. He could have proved it to every individual of His own time and of our time and of all future time. When God wants to prove that the sun and the moon may be depended upon to do their appointed work every day and every night He has no difficulty about it. When He wants to prove that man may depend upon finding the constellations in their places every night—although they vanish and seem lost to us every day—He has no difficulty about it. When He wants to prove that the seasons may be depended upon to come and go according to a fixed law, year after year, He has no difficulty about it. Apparently He has desired to prove to us beyond cavil or doubt many millions of things, and He has had no difficulty about proving them all. It is only when He apparently wants to prove a future life to us that His invention fails and He comes up against a problem which is beyond the reach of His alleged omnipotence. With a message to deliver to men which is of infinitely more importance than all those other messages put together, which He has delivered without difficulty, He can think of no better medium than the poorest of all contrivances—a book. A book written in two languages—to convey a message to a thousand nations—which in the course of the dragging centuries and eons must change and change and become finally wholly unintelligible. And even if they remained fixed, like a dead language, it would never be possible to translate the message with perfect clearness into any one of the thousand tongues, at any time.

According to the hearsay evidence the character of every conspicuous god is made up of love, justice, compassion, forgiveness, sorrow for all suffering and desire to extinguish it. Opposed to this beautiful character—built wholly upon valueless hearsay evidence—it is the absolutely authentic evidence furnished us every day in the year, and verifiable by our eyes and our other senses, that the real character of these gods is destitute of love, mercy, compassion, justice and other gentle and excellent qualities, and is made up of all imaginable cruelties, persecutions and injustices. The hearsay character rests upon evidence only—exceedingly doubtful evidence. The real character rests upon proof—proof unassailable.

Is it logical to expect of gods, whose unceasing and unchanging pastime is the malignant persecution of innocent men and animals, that they are going to provide an eternity of bliss, presently, for these very same creatures? If King Leopold II, the Butcher, should proclaim that out of each hundred innocent and unoffending Congo negroes he is going to save one from humiliation, starvation and assassination, and fetch that one home to Belgium to live with him in his palace and feed at his table, how many people would believe it? Everybody would say "A person's character is a permanent thing. His act would not be in accordance with that butcher's character. Leopold's character *is* established beyond possibility of change and it could never occur to him to do this kindly thing."

Leopold's character is established. The character of the conspicuous gods is also established. It is distinctly illogical to suppose that either Leopold of Belgium or the Heavenly Leopolds are ever going to think of inviting any fraction of their victims to the royal table and the comforts and conveniences of the regal palace.

According to hearsay evidence the conspicuous gods make a pet of one victim in a hundred—select him arbitrarily, without regard to whether he's any better than the other ninety-nine or not—but damn the ninety-nine through all eternity without examining into their case. But for one slight defect this would be logical and would properly reflect the known character of the gods—that defect is the gratuitous and unplausible suggestion that one in a hundred is permitted to pull through. It is not likely that there will be a Heaven hereafter. It is exceedingly likely that there will be a Hell—and it is nearly dead certain that nobody is going to escape it.

As to the human race. There are many pretty and winning things about the human race. It is perhaps the poorest of all the inventions of all the gods but it has never suspected it once. There is nothing prettier than its naive and complacent appreciation of itself. It comes out frankly and proclaims without bashfulness or any sign of a blush that it is the noblest work of God. It has had a billion opportunities to know better, but all signs fail with this ass. I could say harsh things about it but I cannot bring myself to do it—it is like hitting a child.

Man is not to blame for what he is. He didn't make himself. He has no control over himself. All the control is vested in his temperament—which he did not create—and in the circumstances which hedge him round from the cradle to the grave and which he did not devise and cannot change by any act of his will, for the reason that he has no will. He is as purely a piece of automatic mechanism as is a watch, and can no more dictate or influence his actions than can the Watch. He is a subject for pity, not blame—and not contempt. He is flung head over heels into this world without ever a chance to decline, and straightway he conceives and accepts the notion that he is in some mysterious way under obliga-tions to the unknown Power that inflicted this outrage upon him—and thenceforth he considers himself responsible to that Power for every act of his life, and punishable for such of his acts as do not meet with the approval of that Power—yet that same man would argue quite differently if a human tyrant should capture him and put chains upon him of any kind and require obedience: argue that the tyrant had no right to do that; that the tyrant had no right to put commands upon him of any kind and require obedience; that the tyrant had no right to compel him to commit murder and then put the responsibility for the murder upon him. Man constantly makes a most strange distinction between man and his Maker in the matter of morals. He requires of his fellow man obedience to a very creditable code of morals but he observes without shame or disapproval his God's utter destitution of morals.

God ingeniously contrived man in such a way that he could not escape obedience to the laws of his passions, his appetites and his various unpleasant and undesirable qualities. God has so contrived him that all his goings outs and comings in are beset by traps which he cannot pos-sibly avoid and which compel him to commit what are called sins—and then God punishes him for doing these very things which from the begin-ning of time He had always intended that he should do. Man is a machine and God made it—without invitation from any one. Whoever makes a machine here below is responsible for that machine's performance. No one would think of such a thing as trying to put the responsibility upon the machine itself. We all know perfectly well—though we all conceal it, just as I am doing, until I shall be dead and out of reach of public opinion—we all know, I say, that God, and God alone, is responsible for every act and word of a human being's life between cradle and grave. We know it perfectly well. In our secret hearts we haven't the slightest doubt of it. In our secret hearts we have no hesitation in proclaiming as an unthinking fool anybody who thinks he believes that he is by any possibility capable of committing a sin against God—or who thinks he thinks he is under obligations to God and owes Him thanks, reverence and worship.

# NOTES

1. The Chinese philosopher Confucius (551–479 BCE) had expressed what came to be called the Golden Rule, although in negative form: "What I do not wish men to do to me, I also wish not to do to men" (*Analects*, book 5, ch. 11).

2. Charles Augustus Briggs, "Criticism and Dogma," *North American Review* 182 (June 1906): 861–74. Briggs (1841–1913), a Presbyterian minister and professor at the Union Theological Seminary, was a prolific writer on biblical subjects. Twain appears to confuse the Immaculate Conception (referring to the moral purity of the conception of Mary) with the Virgin Birth of Jesus from Mary.

3. Mary Baker Eddy (1821–1910), American religious leader who founded Christian Science with the treatise *Science and Health* (1875).

4. The source of the following newspaper article is unidentified.

5. The Albigenses were a group of Catharist heretics in the south of France in the twelfth, thirteenth, and fourteenth centuries. They suffered a series of massacres from 1022 to 1330.

6. For the St. Bartholomew's Day massacre, see "Man's Place in the Animal World" (p. 153).

7. Leopold II (1835–1909), king of Belgium (1865–1909), gained notoriety for his brutality in treating the natives of the Congo, then a Belgian colony.

8. Alexander VI is unidentified; there has never been any monarch of that name. Twain may be referring to Pope Alexander VI (1431–1503; pope from 1492 to 1503), whose papacy was marred by nepotism, sexual improprieties, and other derelictions.

9. James A. Garfield (1831–1881), president of the United States (1881), was shot by an assassin on July 2, 1881, and lingered for weeks until he died on September 19.

# LITTLE BESSIE
## (1907 or 1908)


### CHAPTER 1


*Little Bessie Would Assist Providence*

*L*ittle Bessie was nearly three years old. She was a good child, and not shallow, not frivolous, but meditative and thoughtful, and much given to thinking out the reasons of things and trying to make them harmonise with results. One day she said—

"Mamma, why is there so much pain and sorrow and suffering? What is it all for?"

It was an easy question, and mamma had no difficulty in answering it:

"It is for our good, my child. In His wisdom and mercy the Lord sends us these afflictions to discipline us and make us better."

"Is it *He* that sends them?"

"Yes."

"Does He send *all* of them, mamma?"

"Yes, dear, all of them. None of them comes by accident; He alone sends them, and always out of love for us, and to make us better."

"Isn't it strange!"

"Strange? Why, no, I have never thought of it in that way. I have not heard any one call it strange before. It has always seemed natural and right to me, and wise and most kindly and merciful."

"Who first thought of it like that, mamma? Was it you?"

"Oh, no, child, I was taught it."

"Who taught you so, mamma?"

"Why, really, I don't know—I can't remember. My mother, I suppose; or the preacher. But it's a thing that everybody knows."

"Well, anyway, it does seem strange. Did He give Billy Norris the typhus?"

"Yes."

"What for?"

"Why, to discipline him and make him good."

"But he died, mamma, and so it *couldn't* make him good."

"Well, then, I suppose it was for some other reason. We know it was a *good* reason, whatever it was."

"What do you think it was, mamma?"

"Oh, you ask so many questions! I think it was to discipline his parents."

"Well, then, it wasn't fair, mamma. Why should *his* life be taken away for their sake, when he wasn't doing anything?"

"Oh, *I* don't know! I only know it was for a good and wise and merciful reason."

"What reason, mamma?"

"I think—I think—well, it was a judgment; it was to punish them for some sin they had committed."

"But *he* was the one that was punished, mamma. Was that right?"

"Certainly, certainly. He does nothing that isn't right and wise and merciful. You can't understand these things now, dear, but when you are grown up you will understand them, and then you will see that they are just and wise."

After a pause:

"Did He make the roof fall in on the stranger that was trying to save the crippled old woman from the fire, mamma?"

"Yes, my child. *Wait!* Don't ask me why, because I don't know. I only know it was to discipline some one, or be a judgment upon somebody, or to show His power."

"That drunken man that stuck a pitchfork into Mrs. Welch's baby when—"

"Never mind about it, you needn't go into particulars; it was to discipline the child—*that* much is certain, anyway."

"Mamma, Mr. Burgess said in his sermon that billions of little creatures are sent into us to give us cholera, and typhoid, and lockjaw, and more than a thousand other sicknesses and—mamma, does He send them?"

"Oh, certainly, child, certainly. Of course."

"What for?"

"Oh, to *dis*cipline us! Haven't I told you so, over and over again?"

"It's awful cruel, mamma! And silly! and if I—"

"Hush, oh *hush!* do you want to bring the lightning?"

"You know the lightning *did* come last week, mamma, and struck the new church, and burnt it down. Was it to discipline the church?"

(Wearily). "Oh, I suppose so."

"But it killed a hog that wasn't doing anything. Was it to discipline the hog, mamma?"

"Dear child, don't you want to run out and play a while? If you would like to—"

"Mamma, only think! Mr. Hollister says there isn't a bird or fish or reptile or any other animal that hasn't got an enemy that Providence has sent to bite it and chase it and pester it, and kill it, and suck its blood and discipline it and make it good and religious. Is that true, mother—because if it is true, why did Mr. Hollister laugh at it?"

"That Hollister is a scandalous person, and I don't want you to listen to anything he says."

"Why, mamma, he is very interesting, and *I* think he tries to be good. He says the wasps catch spiders and cram them down into their nests in the ground—*alive*, mamma!—and there they live and suffer days and days and days, and the hungry little wasps chewing their legs and gnawing into their bellies all the time, to make them good and religious and praise God for His infinite mercies. *I* think Mr. Hollister is just lovely, and ever so kind; for when I asked him if *he* would treat a spider like that, he said he hoped to be damned if be would; and then he—"

"My child! oh, do for goodness' sake—"

"And mamma, he says the spider is appointed to catch the fly, and drive her fangs into his bowels, and suck and suck and suck his blood, to discipline him and make him a Christian; and whenever the fly buzzes his wings with the pain and misery of it, you can see by the spider's grateful eye that she is thanking the Giver of All Good for—well, she's saying grace, as *he* says; and also, he—"

"Oh, aren't you *ever* going to get tired chattering! If you want to go out and play—"

"Mamma, he says himself that all troubles and pains and miseries and rotten diseases and horrors and villainies are sent to us in mercy and kindness to discipline us; and he says it is the duty of every father and mother to *help* Providence, every way they can; and says they can't do it by just scolding and whipping, for that won't answer, it is weak and no good—Providence's way is best, and it is every parent's duty and every *person's* duty to help discipline everybody, and cripple them and kill them, and starve them, and freeze them, and rot them with diseases, and lead them into murder and theft and dishonor and disgrace; and he says Providence's invention for disciplining us and the animals is the very brightest idea that ever was, and not even an idiot could get up anything shinier. Mamma, brother Eddie needs disciplining, right away; and I know where you can get the smallpox for him, and the itch, and the diphtheria, and bone-rot, and heart disease, and consumption, and—*Dear* mamma, have you fainted! I will run and bring help! Now *this* comes of staying in town this hot weather."

## CHAPTER 2

### *Creation of Man*

*Mamma.* You disobedient child, have you been associating with that irreligious Hollister again?

*Bessie.* Well, mamma, he is interesting, anyway, although wicked, and I can't help loving interesting people. Here is the conversation we had:

*Hollister.* Bessie, suppose you should take some meat and bones and fur, and make a cat out of it, and should tell the cat, Now you are not to be unkind to any creature, on pain of punishment and death. And suppose the cat should disobey, and catch a mouse and torture it and kill it. What would you do to the cat?

*Bessie.* Nothing.

*H.* Why?

*B.* Because I know what the cat would say. She would say, It's my nature, I couldn't help it; I didn't make my nature, *you* made it. And so you are responsible for what I've done—I'm not. I couldn't answer that, Mr. Hollister.

*H.* It's just the case of Frankenstein and his Monster over again.[1]

*B.* What is that?

*H.* Frankenstein took some flesh and bones and blood and made a man out of them; the man ran away and fell to raping and robbing and murdering everywhere, and Frankenstein was horrified and in despair, and said, I made him, without asking his consent, and it makes me responsible for every crime he commits. I am the criminal, he is innocent.

*B.* Of course he was right.

*H.* I judge so. It's just the case of God and man and you and the cat over again.

*B.* How is that?

*H.* God made man, without man's consent, and made his nature, too; made it vicious instead of angelic, and then said, Be angelic, or I will punish you and destroy you. But no matter, God is responsible for everything man does, all the same; He can't get around that fact. There is only one Criminal, and it is not man.

*Mamma.* This is atrocious! it is wicked, blasphemous, irreverent, horrible!

*Bessie.* Yes'm, but it's true. And I'm not going to make a cat. I would be above making a cat if I couldn't make a good one.

## CHAPTER 3

Mamma, if a person by the name of Jones kills a person by the name of Smith just for amusement, it's murder, isn't it, and Jones is a murderer?

Yes, my child.

And Jones is punishable for it?

Yes, my child.

Why, mamma?

*Why?* Because God has forbidden homicide in the Ten Commandments, and therefore whoever kills a person commits a crime and must suffer for it.

But mamma, suppose Jones has by birth such a violent temper that he can't control himself?

He *must* control himself. God requires it.

But he doesn't make his own temper, mamma, he is born with it, like the rabbit and the tiger; and so, why should he be held responsible?

Because God *says* he is responsible and *must* control his temper.

But he *can't*, mamma; and so, don't you think it is God that does the killing and is responsible, because it was *He* that gave him the temper which he couldn't control?

Peace, my child! He *must* control it, for God requires it, and that ends the matter. It settles it, and there is no room for argument.

(*After a thoughtful pause.*) It doesn't seem to me to settle it. Mamma, murder is murder, isn't it? and whoever commits it is a murderer? That is the plain simple fact, isn't it?

(*Suspiciously.*) What are you arriving at now, my child?

Mamma, when God designed Jones He could have given him a rabbit's temper if He had wanted to, couldn't He?

Yes.

Then Jones would not kill anybody and have to be hanged?

True.

But He chose to give Jones a temper that would *make* him kill Smith. Why, then, isn't *He* responsible?

Because He also gave Jones a Bible. The Bible gives Jones ample warning not to commit murder; and so if Jones commits it he alone is responsible.

(*Another pause.*) Mamma, did God make the house-fly?

Certainly, my darling.

What for?

For some great and good purpose, and to display His power.

What is the great and good purpose, mamma?

We do not know, my child. We only know that He makes *all* things for a great and good purpose. But this is too large a subject for a dear little Bessie like you, only a trifle over three years old.

Possibly, mamma, yet it profoundly interests me. I have been reading about the fly, in the newest science-book. In that book he is called "the most dangerous animal and the most murderous that exists upon the earth, killing hundreds of thousands of men, women and children every year, by distributing deadly diseases among them." Think of it, mamma, the *most* fatal of all the animals! by all odds the most murderous of all the living things created by God. Listen to this, from the book:

> Now, the house fly has a very keen scent for filth of any kind. When-ever there is any within a hundred yards or so, the fly goes for it to smear its mouth and all the sticky hairs of its six legs with dirt and dis-ease germs. A second or two suffices to gather up many thousands of these disease germs, and then off goes the fly to the nearest kitchen or dining room. There the fly crawls over the meat, butter, bread, cake, anything it can find in fact, and often gets into the milk pitcher, depositing large numbers of disease germs at every step. The house fly is as disgusting as it is dangerous.

Isn't it horrible, mamma! One fly produces fifty-two billions of de-scendants in 60 days in June and July, and they go and crawl over sick people and wade through pus, and sputa, and foul matter exuding from sores, and gaum themselves with every kind of disease-germ, then they go to everybody's dinner-table and wipe themselves off on the butter and the other food, and many and many a painful illness and ultimate death results from this loathsome industry. Mamma, they murder seven thousand persons in New York City alone, every year—people against whom they have no quarrel. To kill without cause is murder—nobody denies that. Mamma?

Well?

Have the flies a Bible?

Of course not.

You have said it is the Bible that makes man responsible. If God didn't give him a Bible to circumvent the nature that He deliberately gave him, God would be responsible. He gave the fly his murderous nature, and sent him forth unobstructed by a Bible or any other restraint to commit murder by wholesale. And so, therefore, God is Himself responsible. God is a murderer. Mr. Hollister says so. Mr. Hollister says God can't make one moral law for man and another for Himself. He says it would be laughable.

*Do* shut up! I wish that that tiresome Hollister was in H—amburg! He is an ignorant, unreasoning, illogical ass, and I have told you over and over again. to keep out of his poisonous company.


# CHAPTER 4

"Mamma, what is a virgin?"

"A maid."

"Well, what is a maid?"

"A girl or woman that isn't married."

"Uncle Jonas says that sometimes a virgin that has been having a child—"

"Nonsense! A virgin can't have a child."

"Why can't she, mamma?"

"Well, there are reasons why she can't."

"What reasons, mamma?"

"Physiological. She would have to cease to be a virgin before she could have the child."

"How do you mean, mamma?"

"Well, let me see. It's something like this: a Jew couldn't be a Jew after he had become a Christian; he couldn't be Christian and Jew at the same time. Very well, a person couldn't be mother and virgin at the same time."

"Why, mamma, Sally Brooks has had a child, and *she's* a virgin."

"Indeed? Who says so?"

"She says so herself."

"Oh, no doubt! Are there any other witnesses?"

"Yes—there's a dream. She says the governor's private secretary appeared to her in a dream and told her she was going to have a child, and it came out just so."

"I shouldn't wonder! Did he say the governor was the corespondent?"

## CHAPTER 5

*B.* Mamma, didn't you tell me an ex-governor, like Mr. Burlap, is a person that's been governor but isn't a governor any more?

*M.* Yes, dear.

*B.* And Mr. Williams said "ex" always stands for a Has Been, didn't he?

*M.* Yes, child. It is a vulgar way of putting it, but it expresses the fact.

*B.* (eagerly). So then Mr. Hollister was right, after all. He says the Virgin Mary isn't a virgin any more, she's a Has Been. He says—

*M.* It is false! Oh, it was just like that godless miscreant to try to undermine an innocent child's holy belief with his foolish lies; and if I could have my way, I—

*B.* But mamma,—honest and true—*is* she still a virgin—a *real* virgin, you know?

*M.* Certainly she is; and has never been anything but a virgin—oh, the adorable One, the pure, the spotless, the undefiled!

*B.* Why, mamma, Mr. Hollister says she *can't* be. That's what *he* says. He says she had five children *after* she had the One that was begotten by absent treatment and didn't break anything and he thinks such a lot of child-bearing, spread over years and years and years, would ultimately wear a virgin's virginity so thin that even Wall street would consider the stock too lavishly watered and you couldn't place it there at any discount you could name, because the Board would say it was wildcat, and wouldn't list it. That's what *he* says. And besides—

*M.* Go to the nursery, instantly! Go!


# CHAPTER 6

Mamma, is Christ God?

Yes, my child.

Mamma, how can He be Himself and Somebody Else at the same time?

He isn't, my darling. It is like the Siamese twins—two persons, one born ahead of the other, but equal in authority, equal in power.

I understand it, now, mamma, and it is quite simple. One twin has sexual intercourse with his mother, and begets himself and his brother; and next he has sexual intercourse with his grandmother and begets his mother. I should think it would be difficult, mamma, though interesting. Oh, ever so difficult. I should think that the Corespondent—

All things are possible with God, my child.

Yes, I suppose so. But not with any other Siamese twin, I suppose. *You* don't think any ordinary Siamese twin could beget himself and his brother on his mother, do you, mamma, and then go on back while his hand is in and beget *her*, too, on his grandmother?

Certainly not, my child. None but God can do these wonderful and holy miracles.

And enjoy them. For of course He enjoys them, or He wouldn't go foraging around among the family like that, *would* He, mamma?— injuring their reputations in the village and causing talk. Mr. Hollister says it was wonderful and awe-inspiring in those days, but wouldn't work now. He says that if the Virgin lived in Chicago now, and got in the family way and explained to the newspaper fellows that God was the

Corespondent, she couldn't get two in ten of them to believe it. He says they are a hell of a lot!

My child!

Well, that is what he says, anyway.

Oh, I do *wish* you would keep away from that wicked, wicked man!

He doesn't *mean* to be wicked, mamma, and he doesn't blame God. No, be doesn't blame Him; he says they all do it—gods do. It's their habit, they've always been that way.

What way, dear?

Going around unvirgining the virgins. He says our God did not invent the idea—it was old and mouldy before He happened on it. Says He hasn't invented anything, but got His Bible and His Flood and His morals and all His ideas from earlier gods, and they got them from still earlier gods. He says there never was a god yet that wasn't born of a Virgin. Mr. Hollister says no virgin is safe where a god is. He says he wishes he was a god; he says he would make virgins so scarce that—

Peace, peace! *Don't* run on so, my child. If you—

—and he advised me to lock my door nights, because—

Hush, *hush*, will you!

—because although I am only three and a half years old and quite safe from *men*—

Mary Ann, come and get this child! There, now, go along with you, and don't come near me again until you can interest yourself in some subject of a lower grade and less awful than theology.

*Bessie.* (disappearing.) Mr. Hollister says there *ain't* any.

## NOTE

1. Mary Shelley's *Frankenstein; or, The Modern Prometheus* (1818) was one of the most popular Gothic novels in the United States.

# THINGS A SCOTSMAN WANTS
# TO KNOW
## (1909)

*Augusta, Maine, August 31.*

To the Editor of Harper's Weekly.

My fellow-townsman, Kaufman, has tried to help the Scotsman. If I may try also, I will do the best I can.

Is, God personal, or impersonal?

Nobody knows; but we can all join the pulpit, and guess. My guess is, that He is personal; that He is supreme, that He is limitlessly powerful, that He is all-knowing, and that He is the Creator of the universe and everything in it.

Is God the author of evil?

Necessarily, since He is the author of the conditions which produce it and make it unavoidable. And inasmuch as He created man—without man's consent or desire—He is responsible for everything man does and says between the cradle and the grave. He has no moral right to dictate to man what his conduct shall be. He has furnished man a large equipment of instincts, partialities, prejudices, magnanimities, generosities, and malignities, and it is man's moral right to do what he pleases with this equipment. As far as God is concerned. He cannot sin against God, he owes Him no allegiance, no obedience. God can compel him, yes, just as a strong man can compel a weak one to do things he is under no contract to do. But He cannot exercise this compulsion without descending a long way below the moral grade of the average civilized human being.

Evil? There is a plenty of it here below—invented in heaven and sent down day and night by the giant cargo and prodigally distributed over an utterly innocent and unoffending world. For what purpose? That bright darling, the pulpit, says, to discipline man, and incline him to love his Maker. What a splendid idea! I doubt if there is a cow in the country that is intellectual enough to invent the match to it.

Every day the cargo comes down, with presents for us all—Christmas all the year round, as it were: cholera, mumps, chills, the Indian Black Death, diphtheria, small pox, scarlet fever, consumption, epilepsy, measles, whooping cough, pneumonia, blindness, lameness, deafness, dumbness, heart failure, apoplexy, hydrophobia, idiocy, insanity, palsy, lockjaw, boils, ulcers, cancers, lumbago, St. Vitus's dance, gout, yellow fever, sleeping sickness, nervous prostration, religion, catalepsy, dropsy, typhoid, malaria, the house-fly, the mosquito, the flea, the louse, appendicitis, meningitis, hunger, cold, poverty, grief, misery in a million forms, and thirty-eight billion hostile microbes in every man's lower intestine waiting to take a chance if the other inducements to holy living fail to catch the student out and hale him to the grave.

Christmas every day, as you see, and something for everybody. Isn't it a wonderful grab-bag? Invented in heaven, too, not in the other place. Have you ever been acquainted with a mere man who would consent to provide any one of these things for the instruction and improvement of his family and friends? Have you ever been acquainted with a mere man who would not be ashamed if you charged him with inflicting any one of them either openly or secretly upon his enemy? If you charged him with it and proved it, and he explained that he did it to make the beneficiary love him, would you let him continue to run at large? The pulpit says God's ways are not our ways. Thanks. Let us try to get along with our own the best we can; we can't improve on them by experimenting with His.

All these horrors are emptied upon man, woman, and helpless child indiscriminately, to discipline them and make them good, and incline them to love their Maker. So the pulpit says. But the like are emptied upon the reptile, the bird, the quadruped and the insect, in the same lavish way. They torture each other, they mutilate each other, they rob each other, they kill each other, they eat each other, they live in the hourly fear of death all their days. Is the idea to train them to righteousness, and make *them* pious, and fit them for heaven?

If it isn't, then what is it for? Why is it done? There is certainly no sense in it, either in their case or man's. Even the cow, with all her intellectual prejudices, will think twice before she disputes that. Then what is it for? Why is it done? It seems to me that it proves one thing conclusively: if our Maker *is* all-powerful for good or evil, He is not in His right mind.

BERUTH A. W. KENNEDY.